STYLISH ENGLISH

STYLISH ENGLISH

Josna Sebastian

Commonwealth

Stylish English

Edition : 2023

ISBN 978-81-311-0243-5

Published by :
COMMONWEALTH PUBLISHERS PVT. LTD.
4831/24, Prahlad Street,
Ansari Road, Darya Ganj,
New Delhi - 110002
Ph. : 23272541, 23257835
Fax : 91- 011- 23257835
e-mail : campusbooks@hotmail.com

Laser Typesetting by :
Dimple Typesetter
Delhi

Printed at :
Roshan Offset Printers
Delhi

Preface

English is referred to as the lingua franca of the modern era. It is the international language in communications, science, aviation, entertainment, and politics. It is an important tool for operating on the world stage. The ability to speak and understand this language is mandatory in certain fields, professions and occupations.

This book *Stylish English* largely focuses on the areas of usage which are often troublesome to non-native speakers of English. Stylish English refers to the writing and setting out of essential information in a way that gives a co-operative, motivated person a good chance of understanding the document at first reading, and in the same sense that the writer meant it to be understood. This means pitching the language at a level of sophistication that suits the readers and using appropriate structure and layout to help them navigate through the document.

This book is an authentic source of information regarding the usage of English stylishly. This book will be highly useful to students, teachers, learners, academics and business professionals.

Josna Sebastian

Contents

1

Stylish Writing of English

Style is synonymous with a set of accepted linguistic conventions; it therefore refers to recommended in-house usage, not to literary style. So 'style' is a matter of everyday concern to both authors and translators. We have tried to bring together much that is available disparately in publications such as the EU Publications Office's Interinstitutional Style Guide, the Commission's Legislative Drafting Guide, the Commission's Legislative Drafting Manual and the interinstitutionally produced Joint Practical Guide for the drafting of EU legislation.

SPELLING

Conventions

- *British spelling*. Follow standard British usage, but remember that influences are crossing the Atlantic all the time (for example, the spellings program and disk have become normal British usage in data processing, while sulfur has replaced sulphur in scientific and technical usage).
- *Words in -ise/-ize*. Use -ise. Both spellings are correct in British English, but the -ise form is

now much more common in the media. Using the -ise spelling does away with the need to list the most common cases where it must be used anyway. (There are up to 40 exceptions to the -ize convention: the lists vary in length, few claiming to be exhaustive.)

— *The -yse form.* The -yse form for such words as paralyse and analyse is the only correct spelling in British English.

— *Digraphs.* Keep the digraph in aetiology, caesium, oenology, oestrogen, etc. (etiology etc. are US usage), but note that a number of such words (e.g. medieval and fetus) are now normally spelt without the digraph in British English. Foetus is still common in Britain in non-technical use.

— *Double consonants.* In British usage (unlike US practice), a final -l is doubled after a short vowel on adding -ing or -ed to verbs (sole exception: parallel, paralleled) and adding -er to make nouns from verbs:

  — travel, travelling, travelled, traveller

  — level, levelling, levelled, leveller

  Other consonants double only if the last syllable of the root verb is stressed or carries a strong secondary stress:

  — admit, admitting, admitted

  — refer, referring, referred

  — format, formatting, formatted

but

— benefit, benefiting, benefited

— focus, focusing, focused

— combat, combating, combated

— target, targeting, targeted

Exception: a few verbs in -p (e.g. handicapped, kidnapped, worshipped, unlike developed).

— *Input/output*. Avoid the forms inputted and outputted; write input and output: e.g. 70 000 records were input last month.

— *Use -ct- not -x- in connection, reflection*, etc. But note complexion and flexion.

— *Write gram, kilogram (not gramme, kilogramme)*. However, use tonne not ton ('ton' refers to the non-metric measure).

— Write *metre* for the unit of length, meter for measuring instruments.

— *Judgment*. The European Courts use the form without the middle -e-, and this practice should be followed for EU purposes.

— *Plurals of words of foreign origin*. Follow the list below.

addendum	addenda
apparatus	apparatus or apparatuses
appendix	appendices (books), appendixes (anatomy)
bacillus	bacilli
bacterium	bacteria
bureau	bureaux
consortium	consortia
corrigendum	corrigenda

criterion	criteria
curriculum	curricula
focus	focuses, focal points, foci (mathematics, science)
formula	formulas (politics) formulae (science)
forum	fora or forums
genus	genera
index	indexes (books), indices (science, economics)
maximum	maximums or maxima
medium	media, mediums (spiritualism)
memorandum	memoranda
papyrus	papyri or papyruses
phenomenon	phenomena
plus	pluses
premium	premiums
referendum	referenda or referendums
spectrum	spectra (science), spectrums (politics)
symposium	symposia or symposiums

Interference Effects

Confusion between English words. Look out for errors involving the pairs below.

dependent (adj. or noun)	dependant (noun only)
license (verb)	licence (noun)
practise (verb)	practice (noun)
principal (adj. or noun)	principle (noun)
stationary (adj.)	stationery (noun)

Confusion between English and French. Beware of interference effects when switching from one language to the other:

French	English
adresse	address
carcasse	carcass or carcase
compétitivité	competitiveness
correspondance	correspondence
existant	existent
indépendance	independence
médecine	medicine
messager	messenger
négligeable	negligible
négociation	negotiation
réflexion	reflection
représentativité	representativeness
responsable	responsible
rincer	rinse
tarif	tariff

Capital Letters

General. Capitalise specific references, but lowercase general references.

As a rule, *capitalise* all nouns and adjectives in names of specific institutions and their subdivisions (directorates-general, directorates, divisions and other departments), committees, working parties and the like:

> Parliament; Council; Commission; Court of Auditors.
> Cereals and Rice Division; Markets in Crop Products

> Directorate.
>
> Permanent Representatives Committee;

In cases where this rule would produce a long series of capitalised words, use discretion, especially where the name of a department, committee or programme reads more like a description of its function than a real title:

> Committee for the adaptation to technical progress of the Directive on the introduction of recording equipment in road transport (tachograph). Joint FAO/EC working party on forest and forest product statistics.

Use *lower case* for *general* references:

> The Court of Justice rules on matters referred to it by courts or tribunals in the Member States. Two separate Commission units are involved. It was decided to set up a number of working parties.

Legislative and other formal instruments. Remember to capitalise specific references but use lower case for general references:

> Regulation (EEC) No 1837/80 (= the Council Regulation of 27 June 1980 or the basic Regulation on sheepmeat); On 29 May 1990, the Council adopted Directive 90/270/EEC on the minimum safety and health requirements for work with display screen equipment.

but:

> It was felt a directive rather than a regulation was the appropriate instrument.

Apply the same rule to title, chapter, section, article and annex in such instruments (including the budget and the Combined Nomenclature - CN).

Official titles. Capitalise the titles of EU (and other) officials and their offices:

> Simone Veil was chosen as first President of the directly elected Parliament in July 1979. The current President of the Council is Prime Minister of Ireland. The Judges and Advocates-General of the Court; President of the First Chamber Director-General for Agriculture; Head of the Road Transport and Inland Waterways Unit.

Note also:

> The meeting opened at 10:00 with Ms Smith presiding. The Chair asked ...

The usage 'Chair' is now the rule in the European Parliament for all its committees.

Political entities. Remember to capitalise specific political entities and to use lowercase when the reference is general, e.g.:

> The French Government
>
> the French authorities, a matter for governments
>
> the State (in political theory and legal texts, otherwise prefer government, as in the role of government, central government, or simply country)
>
> the Member States, nation states, reasons of state, state aid, state-owned, the Arab states (since ill-defined).

International agreements. Follow the same specific/ general rule for treaties, conventions, arrangements, understandings, protocols, etc.

The Treaty of Nice, the International Tin Agreement, the United Nations Protocol against the Smuggling of Migrants

by treaty, under an agreement, the parties agreed to a memorandum of understanding

Permanent and ad hoc bodies. Permanent bodies (e.g. the Commission Delegation in the United States) require capitals, while ad hoc groups (e.g. the Polish delegation to a meeting) do not.

Seasons, etc. No capitals for spring, summer, autumn, winter; capitals for weekdays, months and feast-days (Ascension Day, pre-Christmas business).

Events. Initial capitals throughout for events such as British Week, Love Parade, the International Year of the Child, the Second UN Development Decade. No capitals, however, for the 2003/04 marketing year, the 2004 budget year and so on.

Celestial bodies and objects. Since they are proper nouns, the names of planets, moons, stars and artificial satellites are capitalised (Venus, Rigel, Palapa B). However, the earth, the moon and the sun do not normally take an initial capital unless they are specifically referred to as celestial bodies.

The Starship Enterprise returned to Earth.

but

The daydreamer returned to earth.

Proprietary names. Proprietary names (or trade names) are normally capitalised, unless they have become generic terms, such as aspirin, gramophone, linoleum, nylon, celluloid. Thus, capitalise registered trade names such as Airbus, Boeing, Land Rover, Disprin, Polaroid.

Derivations from proper nouns. When proper nouns are used adjectivally they keep the initial capital (e.g. Bunsen burner, Faraday cage). In the case of words derived from proper nouns (such as pasteurise, quixotic, Rabelaisian), consult a reliable dictionary, as practice varies.

Quotations. Start with a capital in running text only if the quotation is a complete sentence in itself:

> Walther Rathenau once said 'We stand or fall on our economic performance.'
>
> The American Government favours 'a two-way street in arms procurement'.

Geographical Names

General. Many place names have an anglicised form, but as people become more familiar with these names in the language of the country concerned, so foreign spellings will gain wider currency in written English. As a rule of thumb, therefore, use the native form for geographical names except where an anglicised form is overwhelmingly common.

Orthography. Recommended spellings of countries (full names and short forms), country adjectives, capital cities, currencies and abbreviations. Geographical names frequently contain pitfalls for the unwary, particularly in texts dealing with current events. Check carefully that you have used the appropriate English form.

Countries/cities. Watch out for the definite article when translating place names from French, as in the following table.

Country/territory	City/town
(au) Gaza - the Gaza Strip	(à) Gaza - Gaza
(au) Guatemala - Guatemala	(à) Guatemala - Guatemala City
(au) Mexique - Mexico	(à) Mexico - Mexico City
México - Mexico	México D.F. - Mexico City

Scandinavian/Nordic. When referring to the countries of the Nordic Council, i.e. Denmark (including the Faeroes and Greenland), Finland (including Åland), Iceland, Norway and Sweden, use 'Nordic' rather than 'Scandinavian' in terms such as 'Nordic countries' or 'Nordic cooperation'.

However, you may use 'Scandinavia(n)' if you do not need to be specific, though bear in mind the following points. In its narrow geographical interpretation, 'Scandinavia' refers to the two countries of the Scandinavian peninsula, i.e. Norway and Sweden.

In practice, however, it includes Denmark and is often stretched to cover Finland. As a cultural term, 'Scandinavian' also embraces Iceland and the Faeroes. Note that 'Scandinavian languages' refers to the northern Germanic languages, i.e. Danish, Faeroese, Icelandic, Norwegian, and Swedish, but not of course Finnish.

Names of regions. Regional names fall into three types.

- *Administrative units*. Names of units below the top region/province tier should be left in the native spelling, without inverted commas.
- *Traditional geographical names*. Anglicise if the English has wide currency, e.g. the Black Forest,

the Ruhr. Otherwise retain original spelling and accents.

— *Officially designated development areas.* Designated development areas are mostly derived from names of administrative units or from traditional geographical names, often with a defining adjective.

The name of the cross-border region Euregio is written with an initial capital only.

— *Rivers.* Moselle always for wine, and for the river in connection with France and Luxembourg; Mosel may be used if the context is Germany. Use Meuse in French/Belgian contexts, Maas for the Netherlands; Rhine and Rhineland for Rhein, Rhin, Rijn, Rheinland; Tiber for Tevere; Tagus for Tajo/Tejo.

— *Seas.* Anglicise seas (e.g. the Adriatic, the North Sea, the Baltic); Greenland waters implies official sea limits; use 'waters off Greenland' if something else is meant.

— *Lakes.* Anglicise Lake Constance, Lake Geneva, Lake Maggiore. But note

Königssee.

— *Strait/straits.* The singular is the form commonly used in official names, for example: Strait of Dover or Strait of Gibraltar.

— *Other bodies of water.* Write Ijsselmeer (without capital J), Wattenmeer, Kattegat (Danish), Kattegatt (Swedish), Great/Little Belt.

— *Islands.* Islands are often administrative units in their own right, so leave in original spelling, except Corsica, Sicily, Sardinia, the Canary Islands, the Azores and Greek islands with accepted English spellings, such as Crete, Corfu, Lesbos. Use Fyn rather than Fünen in English texts and use West Friesian Islands for Waddeneilanden.

— *Mountains*. Anglicise the Alps, Apennines (one p), Dolomites, Pindus Mountains, and Pyrenees (no accents). Do not anglicise Massif Central (except for capital C), Alpes Maritimes (capital M) or Schwäbische Alb. Alpenvorland should be translated as the foothills of the Alps.

— *Valleys*. Words for valley should be translated unless referring to an official region or local produce: the Po valley, the Valle d'Aosta, Remstal wine.

— *Cities*.

Austria	Use Vienna for Wien.
Belgium	Use the forms Antwerp, Bruges, Brussels, Ghent, Ostend. Flemish v. French forms. Use Flemish names of places in Dutch-speaking provinces and French for French-speaking areas.
Denmark	Note Copenhagen, Aarhus, Aalborg.
Finland	Finland is a bilingual country, and many cities and localities have official names in both Finnish and Swedish. When translating from either language, remember that the form to be used depends on the local

	language situation, not on the text you are translating. A full list of the Finnish/Swedish names which take precedence is kept by the Research Institute for the Languages of Finland. Note in particular that for all major cities the Finnish name must be used:write Helsinki, Oulu, Tampere, Turku, not Helsingfors, Uleåborg, Tammerfors, Åbo.
France	Write Lyon, Marseille, Strasbourg.
Germany	Use the forms Cologne and Munich.
Greece	Use traditional English spellings for well-known cities, regions, islands, etc.—the officially recommended transcription system has not found acceptance even within the European Union and is unknown elsewhere. However, use transliteration for unfamiliar localities, and note that preference should always be given to the demotic forms of place names (where known).
Ireland	Use the English names of cities and towns, except for those in an Irish-speaking area (Gaeltacht).
Italy	Use the English spellings Florence, Genoa, Milan, Naples, Rome, Turin, Venice. Take care not to use the French spelling of other towns, which may differ only slightly from the Italian.

Luxembourg	Use the French spelling for Luxembourg (country and city).
Netherlands	Always write The Hague with a capital T except when used attributively (e.g. the Hague Convention).
Portugal	Use Lisbon.
Spain	Write Seville. Otherwise use Spanish spelling, e.g. Córdoba, La Coruña.
Sweden	Note Gothenburg for Göteborg. However, the Swedish form should be used in some EU-specific contexts, e.g. the Göteborg summit/process.

— *Non-literal geographical names.* Geographical names used in lexicalised compounds tend to be lowercased, as they are no longer considered proper adjectives: roman numerals, gum arabic, prussic acid. Consult an up-to-date reliable dictionary in cases of doubt.

— *Compass points.* No capitals for north, north-west, north-western, etc. unless part of an administrative or political unit or a distinct regional entity. Hence South Africa, Northern Ireland but southern Africa, northern France. Note, however, Central and Eastern European countries (capitalised because the connotations are more political than geographic). Compass bearings are abbreviated without a point (54°E).

— *Compound compass points.* Compound compass points are hyphenated and, in official designations, each part is capitalised (South-

West Germany, the North-West Frontier); always abbreviate as capitals without stops (NW France).

Hyphens and Compound Words

General. Compounds may be written as two or more separate words, or with hyphen(s), or as a single word, and many compounds have followed precisely those steps: data base, data-base, database. One indication of whether words should be joined or separated is stress: underpass is a single word, but under way should be written as two words.

Use hyphens sparingly but to good purpose: the phrase crude oil production statistics needs a hyphen to tell the reader whether 'crude' applies to the oil or to the statistics. Sometimes hyphens are absolutely necessary to clarify the sense:

> re-cover - recover; re-creation - recreation; re-form - reform;
>
> re-count - recount

There are few hard and fast rules, but note the following examples:

> well-known problem; hot-rolled strip; broad-based programme (but a broadly based programme);
>
> oil-bearing rock; user-friendly software;
>
> two-day meeting; four-month stay (but four months' holiday)
>
> balance-of-payments policy; cost-of-living index;
>
> low-interest loans; flood-control measures.

In adverb-adjective modifiers, there is no hyphen when the adverb ends in -ly:

occupationally exposed worker, a beautifully phrased sentence

Many phrases are treated as compounds, and thus need a hyphen, only when used as modifiers:

long-term effects *but* policy for the long term,

large-scale redundancies *but* production on a large scale

Chemical terms. Note that open compounds designating chemical substances do not take a hyphen in attributive position: boric acid solution, sodium chloride powder.

Prefixes are usually hyphenated in recent or ad hoc coinages:

anti-smoking campaign, co-responsibility levies, co-sponsor, ex-army, nonresident, non-flammable, pre-school, quasi-autonomous

If they are of Latin or Greek origin, however, they tend to drop the hyphen as they become established:

antibody, codetermination, codecision, cofinancing, cooperation, subcommittee, subparagraph

Others are more resistant to losing the hyphen:

end-user, end-phase, end-product, all-embracing, all-metal, off-market operations, off-duty

but note

endgame, nonsense, overalls

Nouns from phrasal verbs. These are often hyphenated, but the situation is fluid. Thus handout, takeover, comeback but follow-up, run-up, spin-off.

Present participles of phrasal verbs. When used as attributes they are generally hyphenated:

cooling-off period;

Avoiding double consonants and vowels. Hyphens are often used to avoid juxtaposing two consonants or two vowels:

aero-elastic, anti-intellectual, part-time, re-election, re-entry, re-examine

However, the hyphen is often omitted in frequently used words:

bookkeeping, coeducation, cooperation, coordinate, macroeconomic, microeconomic, radioactive.

Numbers and fractions. Numbers take hyphens when they are spelled out. Fractions take hyphens when used attributively, but not when used as nouns:

twenty-eight, two-thirds completed

BUT

an increase of two thirds.

Prefixes before proper names. Prefixes before proper names are hyphenated: pro-American, intra-Community, mid-Atlantic, pan-European, trans-European. Note, however, that transatlantic is written solid.

Coordination of compounds. Hyphenated compounds may be coordinated as follows:

gamma- and beta-emitters, acid- and heat-resistant, hot- and cold-rolled products

Where compounds are not hyphenated (closed compounds), or should you choose to write them so, they should not be coordinated but written out in full:

> macrostructural and microstructural changes, minicomputers and microcomputers, prenatal and postnatal effects, agricultural inputs and outputs
>
> NOT
>
> macro- and microstructural changes, mini- and microcomputers, pre- and postnatal effects, agricultural in- and outputs
>
> (BUT of course
>
> macro- and micro-structural changes, pre- and post-natal effects)

Closed compounds in technical texts. Some expressions that are written as separate words in everyday language become closed compounds in more specialist contexts, e.g. pigmeat, longwall. This reflects the fact that in a particular field such expressions have the status of precise terms.

PUNCTUATION

The punctuation in an English text must follow the rules and conventions for English, which often differ from those applying to other languages. Note in particular that:

— punctuation marks in English are always - apart from dashes and ellipsis points - closed up to the preceding word;

— stops (. ? ! : ;) are always followed by only a single (not a double) space;

— quotation marks may be either straight ('...') or preferably smart ('...'), but not both in the same text, and never chevrons («...») or as in German („...").

Full Stop

No further full stop is required if a sentence ends with an abbreviation that takes a point (e.g. 'etc.') or with a quotation complete in itself that ends in a full stop, question mark or exclamation mark before the final quotes:

> René Descartes said 'I think therefore I am.'

Full stops as omission marks (aka ellipsis points). Always use three points, preceded by a hard space. In Word, use Alt + Ctrl + (full stop) to insert ellipsis points. In French texts the points are commonly enclosed in brackets. This is never done in English:

> 'The objectives of the Union shall be achieved ... while respecting the principle of subsidiarity.'

If a sentence ends with an omission, no fourth full stop should be added. If any other punctuation mark follows, there is no space before it.

Run-in side heads (you are looking at one). These are followed by a stop in English typographical practice (while colons are used in French).

Colon

— Colons are most often used to indicate that an expansion, qualification or explanation is about to follow (e.g. a list of items in running text). The part before the colon must be a full sentence in its own right, but the second need not be.

- Do not use colons at the end of headings.
- Colons do not require the next word to start with a capital: contrast usage in German etc.
- Colons should be closed up to the preceding word, unlike in French usage.

Semicolon

Use a semicolon rather than a comma to combine two sentences into one without a linking conjunction:

> The committee dealing with the question of commas agreed on a final text; however, the issue of semicolons was not considered.

You may also use semicolons instead of commas to separate items in a series, especially phrases that themselves contain commas.

Semi-colons should be closed up to the preceding word, unlike in French usage.

Comma

Items in a series. Here, the comma may be considered to stand for a missing 'and' or 'or'.

> John mowed the lawn, Mary did the cooking and Frank lazed around.
>
> He came, saw and conquered.
>
> The committee considered sugar, beef and milk products.

Insert an additional comma before the final 'and' (or 'or') if needed for clarification:

> sugar, beef and veal, and milk products.

A comma also comes before 'etc.' in a series:

> sugar, beef, milk products, etc.

but not if no series is involved:

> They discussed milk products etc., then moved on to sugar.

Commas also divide adjectives in series:

> moderate, stable prices.

but not if the adjectives do not form a series:

> stable agricultural prices.

In the second example, 'stable' modifies 'agricultural prices', i.e. the phrase cannot be read as 'stable and agricultural prices'.

Linked sentences. Use a comma to separate two sentences linked by a conjunction such as 'but', 'yet', 'while' or 'so' to form a single sentence:

> The committee dealing with the question of commas agreed on a final text, but the issue of semicolons was not considered.

Where there is no conjunction, use a semicolon

Parenthetic and introductory phrases. If a phrase is intended to complement or introduce the information in a sentence and has a separate emphasis of its own, it is set off by a comma, or by a pair of commas if inside the sentence:

> Mindful of the need to fudge the issue, the committee on commas never came to a conclusion.
>
> The committee on commas is composed of old fogeys, as you know.

> The committee on commas, however, was of a different opinion.

Note that the sentence must remain a complete sentence even if the parenthetic or introductory phrase is omitted.

Parenthetic phrases may also be created by setting off part of the sentence with a comma (or commas) while retaining the normal word order. Both the following are possible:

> The President was a great man despite his flaws.
>
> The President was a great man, despite his flaws.

Without the comma, the phrase 'despite his flaws' forms part of the statement. With the comma, the phrase complements it, i.e. the sentence retains its sense if the phrase is omitted. The comma is therefore correctly left out in the following sentence:

> Phrases must not be set off by commas if this changes the intended meaning of the sentence.

However, a comma is required if the phrase has a separate emphasis simply by virtue of being moved out of position, for example to the beginning of the sentence:

> If this changes the intended meaning of the sentence, phrases must not be set off by commas.

Note, though, that short introductory phrases need not have any separate emphasis of their own, i.e. they may be run into the rest of the sentence. Both the following are possible:

> In 2003, the committee took three decisions.
>
> In 2003 the committee took three decisions.

Parenthetic phrases (but not introductory phrases) may sometimes be marked by dashes or brackets.

Non-defining relative clauses. Non-defining relative clauses are special cases of parenthetic phrases. Note the difference compared with relative clauses that define the preceding noun phrase (i.e. 'the translations' or 'the translation in the tray' in the examples below):

> The translations, which have been revised, can now be sent out.
>
> (added detail - they have all been revised)
>
> The translations which (or better: that) have been revised can now be sent out.
>
> (defining the subset that is to be sent out - only those that have been revised are to be sent out)

Note also that the use of 'which' in defining relative clauses is often considered to be stilted and overly formal. 'That' reads more naturally. It also helps make the meaning clearer, reinforcing the lack of commas, since it is used as a relative pronoun only in defining clauses. Unlike 'which', however, 'that' needs to be close to the noun to which it refers.

Combined uses of commas. The uses of commas described above can of course be combined. Worth noting is that an initial comma is not needed before introductory phrases in linked sentences:

> The committee dealing with the question of commas agreed on a final text, but despite the importance of the matter, the relationship with semicolons was not considered.

Avoiding commas. Avoid liberally sprinkling sentences with commas, but do so by constructing sentences so as to minimise the number of commas required rather than by breaching the comma rules described above. For example, inserted phrases can often be moved to the beginning of the sentence.

Parenthetic phrases can also be rendered with brackets or dashes. Moreover, a parenthetic phrase may not in fact be appropriate. Finally, a complex sentence can be divided by a semicolon or even split into two or more sentences.

Dashes

Dashes v hyphens. Most users of word processors do not distinguish between dashes and hyphens, using hyphens to represent both short dashes ('en' dashes = -) and long dashes ('em' dashes = -) commonly used in typeset documents. However, please note that both en and em dashes are available in modern word processors.

Em dashes may be used to punctuate a sentence instead of commas or round brackets. They increase the contrast or emphasis of the text thus set off. However, use no more than one in a sentence, or—if used with inserted phrases—one set of paired dashes. To avoid errors if your dashes subsequently turn into hyphens as a result of document conversion, do not follow the typesetting practice of omitting the spaces around the em dashes. In Microsoft Word, the keyboard shortcut for the em dash is Alt + Ctrl + - (on the numeric keypad).

En dashes are used to join coordinate or contrasting pairs (the Brussels-Paris route, a current-voltage graph, the height-depth ratio). These are not subject to hyphen rules. In Microsoft Word, the keyboard shortcut for the en dash is Ctrl + - (on the numeric keypad).

Brackets

Round brackets. Also known as parentheses, round brackets are used much like commas, except that the text they contain has a lower emphasis. They are often used to expand on or explain the preceding item in the text:

> ARZOD (an employment service) is based in Ruritania.

Round brackets in citations. Use a pair of round brackets when citing numbered paragraphs from legal instruments, and close up to the article number:

> Article 3(1), Article 3(1)(a), Article 3a(1), etc.

Bracketed sentences. A whole sentence in brackets should have the final stop inside the closing bracket. Do not forget the stop at the end of the preceding sentence as well.

Square brackets. Square brackets are used to make insertions in quoted material. They are also used by convention in administrative drafting to indicate optional passages or those still open to discussion, so do not replace with round brackets.

When translating, also use square brackets to insert translations or explanations after names or titles left in the original language.

Question Mark

Courtesy questions. No question mark is needed after

a request or instruction put as a question for courtesy:

> Would you please sign and return the attached form.

Do not use a question mark in indirect speech:

> The chairman asked when the deadline would be fixed.

Question marks should be closed up to the preceding word, unlike in French usage.

Exclamation Mark

In English, exclamation marks are used solely to mark exclamations, such as 'How we laughed!' or 'What a fiasco!', or to add exclamatory force to a statement, e.g. 'Two million cows had to die!', or a command, e.g. 'Please read this paragraph!'.

Exclamatory expressions are appropriate in texts that directly address the reader or audience, such as speeches or informal instructions, but are usually out of place in formal texts. Note that exclamation marks are not used to mark the imperative as such in English.

Factorials. As a mathematical symbol, the exclamation mark identifies a factorial:

$$6! = 6 \times 5 \times 4 \times 3 \times 2 \times 1$$

Exclamation marks should be closed up to the preceding word, unlike in French usage.

Quotation Marks

— *Double v single quotation marks.* Use single quotation marks to signal direct speech and verbatim quotes, and double quotation marks for quotations within these. You may also use single quotation marks to identify words and phrases that are not themselves quotes but to which you wish to draw attention as lexical items.

— *Short quotations.* Short quotes of up to four lines or thereabouts are normally run into the surrounding text. They are set off by opening and closing quotation marks only.

— *Block quotations.* Extended (block) quotations should be indented and separated from the surrounding text by paragraph spacing before and after. No quotation marks are required with this distinctive layout.

— *English text in source documents.* An English text quoted in a foreign language text keeps the quotation marks in the English target text. But if a single English word or phrase is put in quotation marks simply to show that it is a foreign element, the quotation marks should be removed.

— *Back-translating of quotes.* Avoid if possible. However, if you cannot find the original English version, turn the passage into indirect speech without quotation marks. The same applies where the author has applied quotation marks to a non-verbatim reference.

— *So-called.* Quotation marks are preferable to so-called, which has pejorative connotations, to render soi-disant, sogenannt, etc.

— *Other uses.* Generally, use quotation marks as sparingly as possible for purposes other than actual quotation.

French and German authors tend to make frequent use of inverted commas for nouns in apposition (often programme or committee names etc.), as in le Conseil 'Agriculture' or Komitee 'Menschliche Faktoren'. It is usually preferable to omit the quotation marks in English and reverse the order:

> the Agriculture Council, the Human Factors Committee, etc.

Apostrophe

Possessive of nouns. The possessive form of nouns is marked by an apostrophe followed by an -s. After the plural ending 's', however, the possessive -s is omitted:

> the owner's car
>
> women's rights
>
> footballers' earnings

Note that the apostrophe is never used in possessive adjectives:

> its (as distinct from it's, i.e. 'it is'), ours, theirs, yours

Nouns ending in -s, including proper names and abbreviations, form their singular possessive with -'s, just like nouns ending in other letters.

> an actress's pay; Mr Jones's paper;
>
> Helios's future is uncertain; AWACS's success

The -s after terminal s' used to be omitted in written English, but this is now done only in classical and biblical names, e.g. Socrates' philosophy, Xerxes' fleet.

Note that some place names also omit the apostrophe (Earls Court, Kings Cross). Possessives of proper names in titles sometimes omit the apostrophe as well. There is no apostrophe in Achilles tendon.

Contractions. Apostrophes are also used to indicate contractions, i.e. where one or more letters have been omitted in a word or where two words have been joined together. Contractions are common in informal texts, but not in formal texts. Examples:

don't = do not

it's = it is (as distinct from the possessive 'its')

who's = who is (as distinct from whose)

you're = you are (as distinct from your)

Plurals of abbreviations. Plurals of abbreviations (MEPs, OCTs, SMEs, UFOs, VDUs) do not take an apostrophe.

Plurals of figures. Plurals of figures do not take an apostrophe:

Pilots of 747s undergo special training.

Plurals of single letters. The plurals of single lowercase letters may, however, take an apostrophe to avoid misunderstanding:

Dot your i's.

Mind your p's and q's.

In tables, write '000 tonnes (or of course thousand tonnes or thousands of tonnes), not in 1 000 tonnes.

NUMBERS

General. In deciding whether to write numbers in words or figures, the first consideration should be consistency within a passage. As a general rule write low numbers (up to nine inclusive) in words and larger numbers (10 and above) in figures. If the passage contains both kinds, however, use either figures or words for all the numbers.

Always use figures with units of measurement that are denoted by symbols or abbreviations:

EUR 50 or fifty euros

250 kW or two hundred and fifty kilowatts

205 μg or two hundred and five micrograms

5ºC or five degrees Celsius

The converse does not hold. If the units of measurement are spelled out, the numbers do not also have to be spelled out but may be written with figures: *250 kilowatts, 500 metres.*

With hundred and thousand there is a choice of using figures or words:

300 or three hundred but not 3 hundred

EUR 3 000 or three thousand euros but not EUR 3 thousand

Million and billion, however, may be combined with figures:

2.5 million, 3 million, 31 billion

Writing out Numbers

As a rule, avoid combining single-digit figures and words using hyphens (a 2-hour journey) but write out instead:

a three-year period; a five-door car

But note set phrases such as:

40-hour week, 24-hour clock, 4-wheel drive

When two numbers are adjacent, spell out one of them:

90 fifty-gram weights, seventy 25-cent stamps

Compound numbers that are to be written out (e.g. in treaty texts) take a hyphen:

the thirty-first day of December, nineteen hundred and eighty-one

Grouping of thousands. Do not use either commas or points but insert protected spaces (4 000 000). Note that serial numbers are not grouped in thousands.

In tables write:

EUR '000 or EUR thousand, but not in EUR 1 000.

'000 tonnes or thousand tonnes or thousands of tonnes, but not in 1 000 tonnes

Billion. The use of billion to designate thousand million (rather than million million) is now officially recognised by the Commission and is standard usage in official EU publications. Leading British newspapers and journals (such as the Financial

Times and The Economist) have also adopted the convention.

Abbreviating 'million' and 'billion'. Do not use mio. The letters m and bn can be used for sums of money to avoid frequent repetitions of million, billion; this applies particularly in tables where space is limited. The abbreviation should be closed up to the figure (examples: €230m, £370m, $230bn).

Fractions

Written out. Insert hyphens in fractions used as adverbs or adjectives but not if they are nouns:

> a two-thirds increase, but an increase of two thirds.

Avoid combining figures and words:

> two-thirds completed, not 2/3 completed

Decimal points. When translating, do not replace commas with points in legislation (including the budget). This was agreed in the 1970s by the UK and Irish Permanent Representatives. The same goes for all other work that is to appear in the Official Journal of the European Union. Elsewhere, replace decimal commas with points.

Note when quoting statistics that 3.5 (as in 3.5%) is not the same as 3.50 or 3½; each decimal place, even if zero, adds to the precision. The non-decimal fraction is more approximate.

Ranges

Written out. When a range is written out, repeat symbols and multiples (i.e. thousand, million, etc.):

from EUR 20 million to EUR 30 million

between 10ºC and 70°C

Abbreviated form. When a range is indicated by a dash (N.B. use an en-dash), do not repeat the symbol or multiple if they do not change and close up the dash between the figures:

€20-30 million, 10-70ºC

If the symbol or multiple changes, however, leave a blank space on either side of the dash:

100 kW - 40 MW

Dates and Time

Dates

Write out the month, preceded by a simple figure for the day, e. g. 23 July 1997. Use all four digits when referring to specific years (i.e. 1997 not '97). However, in footnotes and where space is at a premium, the month can be written as a number.

Note that in American usage, 23 July 1997 is 7.23.97 and in the international dating system it is 1997-07-23.

Avoiding redundancy. If the year in question is absolutely clear from the context, the year number may be left out: on 23 July 2001, the Committee adopted... but subsequently on 2 August, it decided...

Decades. When referring to decades write the 1990s (no apostrophe).

Systems of chronology. The letters AD come before the year number (AD 2000), whereas BC follows it (347 BC). CE (Common Era), BCE (Before Common Era) and BP (Before Present) also follow the year number.

Time spans. Use a closed-up dash. For the second figure, you should not repeat the century if it is the same, but you should always include the decade:

> 1870-1901, 1905-10, 1914-18, 1939-45, 1980-86, 1996-2006

Note the following patterns:

> from 1990 to 1995 (not: from 1990-95)
>
> between 1990 and 1995 (not: between 1990-95)
>
> 1990 to 1995 inclusive (not: 1990-95 inclusive)

Note that 1990-91 is two years. Single marketing years, financial years, etc. that do not coincide with calendar years are denoted by a forward slash: e.g. 1990/91, which is twelve months or less.

Time

Use the 24-hour system in preference to the 12-hour system.

When writing times, use a colon in preference to a point between hours and minutes, without adding hrs or o'clock: 11:30. However, if the original document uses a point, this may be retained for the sake of convenience.

For midnight either write the word midnight or use 24:00 (for periods ending then) or 00:00 (for periods starting then).

For duration use h:

the time allowed for the test is 2½ h.

Distinguish summertime (the season) from summer time, e.g. British Summer Time (BST).

ABBREVIATIONS, ACRONYMS AND SYMBOLS

Abbreviations and Acronyms

General. As a general principle, abbreviations, acronyms and symbols should be used as much for the convenience of the reader as of the writer. Overuse will baffle and irritate most readers.

Acronyms are normally uppercased. However, if an acronym has come to be regarded as a proper name, it retains only an initial capital. This requires it to conform to the rules for English spelling, to be pronounced as a normal word and to carry no risk of confusion with an existing word.

As a rule, the longer the acronym, the more likely it is to lose its capitals. To ensure consistency and remove the need for subjective decisions, follow the 'five-letter' rule in 4.2 below. Bear in mind, though, that this rule is necessarily arbitrary. Finally, ignore the convention in many online databases of uppercasing all acronyms and abbreviations.

Longer acronyms. Lowercase those with more than five letters, with initial capital, provided they can be pronounced. Thus:

Benelux, Esprit, Helios, Interreg, Resider, Unesco, Unctad but: EFILWC, EMCDDA, etc.

Computer terms are also exceptions:

FORTRAN, WYSIWYG

Short acronyms. Five letters or fewer: uppercase throughout without points:

ACP, BSE, EAGGF, EEA, EIB, ERDF, FADN, ISDN, OECD, R&D (no spaces!), UNHCR

and, though pronounceable: AIDS, COST, ECHO, EFTA, NASA, NATO, SHAPE, TRIPS

But note: the EU programmes Tacis and Phare are no longer considered to be acronyms.

Indefinite article. Apply the rule 'a before consonant, an before vowel' as if a following abbreviation is being spoken:

a UN resolution/an Unctad meeting, an EDF project

a NATO decision, an MP

Plurals of abbreviations. Plurals of abbreviations do not take an apostrophe:

SMEs, UFOs, VDUs, OCTs

Lowercase or mixed-case abbreviations. There is a small but high-frequency class of abbreviations that traditionally are written in lowercase (including at the beginning of a sentence in footnotes) and require points after each letter, such as e.g., i.e. No comma is required after them but one should be used before if they are part of a list. Do not use e.g. and etc. in the same list.

Most other lowercase and mixed-case abbreviations are written without stops: aka, fob, cif, BAe (British Aerospace), etc., including most scientific abbreviations and symbols: pH, etc.

Single truncated words. Single truncated words take a point unless the last letter is included:

> Jan., Sun., Co., fig., etc., cf., chap., cp., dict., ibid.
>
> Mr, Mrs, Dr, Fr (Father), Ltd, Pty, St Petersburg

Abbreviate 'number' as No (plural Nos), which has no final stop as it is derived from Latin numero.

Single letters. Single letters (uppercase or lowercase) conventionally take a point. Exceptions: scientific symbols (chemical elements, basic and derived units, etc.) and the v in the names of court cases and sporting contests.

First names should be abbreviated with a single initial only (Philippe: P., Theodor: T.). For compound first names, use both initials (Jean-Marie: J-M).

Note also: p. = page (plural: pp.); l. = line, (plural: ll.)

Foreign-language abbreviations. Untranslated foreign-language abbreviations should retain the capitalisation and punctuation conventions of the original (e.g. GmbH).

Abbreviate Nota Bene as NB not N.B.

Mathematical Symbols

— *Per cent*. Note that per cent is normally written as two words in British English. Use per cent where the number is also spelled out in words: twenty per cent. With figures, use the per cent sign (%). In English, the sign is always closed up to the figure.

— *Percentages*. Express percentage relationships in running text economically, especially when translating: un taux de 65% par rapport à la totalité des exportations en dehors de l'Union européenne translates simply as 65% of EU exports.

— *Technical tolerances*. Do not use ± (ASCII 241) to mean 'about' or 'approximately'. Use it only for technical tolerances.

— *Foreign-language conventions*. Remember that languages may have different conventions as regards their use of mathematical signs.

— *Open dashes*. Use a closed-up dash, not a hyphen or open dash to signify a range (e.g. 10-12%).

— *Multiplication sign*. Change points used as a multiplication sign to 'x' or '*', e.g. 2.6. 1018 becomes 2.6 x 10^{18} or 2.6 * 10^{18}.

Scientific Symbols And Units of Measurement

— *General*. Most scientific symbols in current use are interlingual forms and do not require any adaptation when writing in English. In the specific case of weights and measures, the International System of Units (SI - Système International) has now been adopted almost universally for science and technology, as well as generally for trade and industry in the EU.

— *Names of units of measurement*. Names of basic and derived units of measurement are always lowercased even if they are derived from a personal name, e.g. ampere, kelvin, hertz, newton, pascal, watt, siemens, becquerel.

They have normal plurals in -s: 250 volts, 50 watts, etc. Note that proper names used adjectivally retain their initial capital: Richter scale, Mach number, degree Celsius.

- *Degree sign*. The degree sign in temperatures and compass bearings, e.g. 25°C or 65°NE, is closed up on both sides.
- *Symbols for units of measurement*. These are normally abridged forms of the names of these units. They are written without stops, are not closed up to figures and do not have plurals (4 ha, 9 m, 60 km, 50 km/h, 200 g, 5 kg, 40 t, 20 bar, 55 dB (A), 2 000 kc/s).
- *Ohm*. The ohm symbol is capital omeg. All other SI symbols for units of measurement are formed from unaccented Latin characters.
- *Internal capitals*. Symbols for units of measurement that start with a capital letter keep the capital internally when used with a prefix: kHz, MHz, eV, etc. When combining prefixes with units, link either symbols only or full-forms only: thus kilohertz or kHz but not kiloHz or khertz.
- *Capitalisation/lowercasing of symbols*. The initial letter of symbols for SI units derived from personal names is always capitalised: Hz (hertz), Bq (becquerel), N (newton), K (kelvin), etc. Symbols derived from generic nouns are always lowercased and are the same for both singular and plural: g (gram), kg (kilogram), lm (lumen), lx (lux), mol (mole), cd (candela), etc.
- *Non-SI units of measurement*. Some non-metric units of measurement are still permitted for certain purposes, e.g. the pint in Ireland and the

UK and miles and yards in the UK. Greece uses the stremma (1 000 square metres) for land measurement. Aircraft altitudes are often expressed in feet (ft). Do not convert quantities, although an explanatory footnote may be inserted if appropriate.

- *Computing*. Where computers are concerned, K (kilo), M (mega) and G (giga) often stand for binary thousands (1 024=2^10), millions (1 048 576=2^20) and billions (1 073 741 824=2^30), respectively. Note the capital K in this usage.
- *Electric power*. Kilowatt (kW) and megawatt (MW) are used for generating capacity, kWh and MWh for output over a given period.
- *Chemical elements*. The names of the chemical elements start with a lowercase letter, including elements whose designations are derived from proper names: californium, einsteinium, nobelium, etc. Their symbols (which are interlingual) consist either of a single capital or a capital and small letter (N, Sn, U, Pb, Mg, Z) without a point.
- In shipping, grt stands for gross register tonnage (not registered) and gt for gross tonnage.

2

Stylish English Conversation

Why can't one stand with confidence and speak exactly what is required to be said? Why is the sentence "I am not confident of my English" the most common sentence we hear in India whenever you talk of "lack of confidence?" Why is it that whatever many of you speak has so much of Hindi in it that the language sounds more like Hinglish than English? Why are sentences an amalgamation of lots of words that *almost* mean what you want to say and not *exactly* what you want to say?

Where is the problem?

- Every one knows what is to be said but *do not know how to say it.*
- Have the fear of speaking Wrong English.
- *Fear* leads to *lack of confidence,* because of which one is unable to converse in English, in public.

The obvious Solution is:

- Understanding Grammar rules.
- Learning New words (daily usage words)
- Learning from the dictionary, at least one word a day.

- Learning to Express in English.
- Decoding a perception or a thought in English.
- Public Speaking
- Understanding the Language change in the corporate world.
- Learning how the same conversation has to be *formalized in the corporate culture.*

Yes, you all know what is to be done but little do we realise as to how it is to be done?

USE OF ENGLISH

English is one of the most flexible and expressive languages in the world. Its immense vocabulary provides for the precise and persuasive communication of ideas. It is a language of subtle verbal inflections, which enable the writer to project mood and emotion, to formulate thought and principle with clarity and impact.

But the very richness of English makes it difficult to use well. If there are always so many ways of saying something, how can you be sure you have chosen the right one?

The obvious doubts are:

- Should I write in formal English as I speak?
- Should I use long, impressive phrases or short, expressive ones?
- What about American or British English?

Spoken English and written Business English are two different approaches. Whether you speak big words or not, is not the point, the idea is that you must be able to convey exactly what you wish to. And more importantly the listener must interpret exactly what you want him to understand.

The best advice is to write for your reader and speak for your listener. You should use a clear form of English, avoiding jargon or slang. To take you ahead, to succeed in the Corporate World, and to be able to speak Correct English and that too effectively and confidently, there are a few things you need to understand very clearly:

a) All those who always said that," *you must talk in English, with your friends and family...* and wherever you go and whatever you do, *think in English*", were actually correct.

b) You have to work towards killing that fear or the discomfort attached to speaking English. This you can only do by *speaking* English.

c) Please do not worry; if you are speaking wrong English, It does not matter as long as you are in the learning stage. All you need to do is, *kill the fear.*

d) The idea of talking about your most favorite dream or aspiration; or even arguing, or fighting in English at a stretch for about a minute can help you get rid of fear, provided you *continue the exercise.*

e) Many of us try to learn a few words looking into the dictionary.

f) Another way of speaking better and refined English is to use *"better synonyms"*. Why call a canteen a canteen when you can call it a Cafeteria!

g) *Confidence!* Be it English or any other Language, needs to be spoken with confidence.

What follows now is a *combination of rules and tips* to be followed to help you improve your conversational abilities. Good English Conversation is a combination of correct English and conversation abilities.

CONVERSATION

The kind of skills needed for a full conversation in English go some way beyond replying to the question. It's about keeping people company, not something immediately associated with business in this culture.

> If small talk is the warm-up, conversation is the full workout.

Conversation is about making others comfortable by continuing to talk to them. So keep it going, even if the subject matter is not exactly up your street.

The essence of English conversation lies in flexibility and humour. So finish your point smartly and ask for their opinion.

> Talk to a man about himself, and he will speak for hours.

Simplify your sentence structure and vocabulary

This is particularly important for English speakers who the ability to use complex grammatical structures.

Beware of the differences between the various versions of English British & American.

Learn the art of "Small Talk"

The first thing you should know here is that the word small in small talk has nothing to do with size. There is nothing unimportant about small talk. It is "light social conversation".

You should know that small talk is a vital positive signal in business. It normally opens the communication.

Interpersonal skills

In English, many of these skills are expressed in handy phrases, which generate feel good factor. They may be missing from your vocabulary.

— Be polite and reject an apology with 'No need to apologize'.

— Don't wish them a cold and final 'Goodbye'. Relax the flesh with a casual 'Take care'.

— Wish your partner a pleasant journey home with 'Safe trip home'. And don't forget to ask for their friends: 'Give my regards to one and all'.

Introduce

Make sure you can introduce yourself. The best way is often just to say your name, job and company: "Hello. Tanvi Singh. I'm the marketing manager at P&G."

In many situations, however, we make small talk without introducing ourselves at all. Imagine that you are visiting a company in London and someone says to you in the lift: "Nice weather, isn't it?" In this encounter, it would be ridiculous to start by saying: "Good morning, Tanvi Singh. I'm the marketing manager at P&G." *And never ever say " Myself, Tanvi Singh"* Sadly this is quite a popular mistake that people in India commit while introducing themselves.

Yes, you are right, the weather is nice." Instead, you must typically reply: "Yes, lovely, isn't it?"

Be open

One of the most important skills during small talk is the ability to keep the conversation going. One way to do this is to ask *open questions,* which require your partner in conversation to answer with more than "yes" or "no". Practice using open questions - those that start with "when", "where", "how", "how long" etc. For example: "What do you think of Delhi so far?"

Give feedback, add information

As the listener in a conversation, you can encourage the speaker by giving feedback - with expressions such as "I see", "oh, that's interesting" or "right". In small talk, silence is definitely not golden. Listeners can also help to make conversation more fluid by adding extra information. For example, if you are asked a closed question such as "is your hotel alright?", then you could say, "yes, thank you, it's very comfortable, and the service has been excellent".

Classic topics

There are a number of classic topics for business small talk, and you should make sure you have the vocabulary to talk about them. These include:

- Health (for example, "how have you been recently?"),
- Travel ("how was your flight?")
- Accommodation ("how is your hotel?")
- Family ("how old are your children now?")
- Holidays ("where did you go on holiday this year?")
- The weather ("how's the weather been here recently?").

Keep small talk small

It is sometimes said that, in light conversation, "the British talk about the weather, the Germans talk about their health". But remember that your business partners do not want to hear a detailed report of your medical troubles!

Saying goodbye can be as awkward as saying hello. Once again, keep it simple, but polite. For example: "It was very nice to meet you", or "It was nice seeing you again". The answer to such comments is simple: "Pleasure."

Ways to start a good conversation

"I noticed..."

"Tell me..."

"I appreciate..."

"What do you think..." or, "I need some advice..."

"Why do you say that..."

- *"Don't bring anger into a conversation* — anger is one letter short of danger. To be effective, you have to be patient. Don't send the other party the wrong cues. Body language, direct eye contact, open honesty and a healthy positive attitude go a long way."

- *"Listening is very important to proper communication.* Listen first and then reply in the same business manner of the person you are communicating with. Watch the person you are communicating with for signs of understanding.
- The most important way to avoid barriers is to listen to the other person. Most people are nervous – they want to get what they need to say out and get the situation over with (myself included). If you go in and listen, you can often identify the other person's position on the matter and adjust your reply accordingly.

Six common corporate conversation faux pas

Arriving empty-headed

"People walk into an event, a room full of strangers, and they don't know what to talk about,"

Few of us are good at ad-libbing, and it shows when we're trying to make sparkling conversation. The usual result: flat talk of your business or repeating yourself because you've run out of topics to discuss. Instead, select some conversation subjects before you head to the party. *"It's important to have a variety of topics."*

Assuming everyone's acquainted

Presuming that you're the only person at the party who doesn't know anyone can have dire consequences.

People who think that way usually beat a hasty retreat, hiding behind a plant or staying on the sidelines. Such behavior will at best make you come across as shy; at worst, you'll look like a party pooper. Fix this faux pas by assuming that nobody knows anybody. "Walk into the room and assume that people want to meet you. That's why people come to parties, to socialise.

If you keep your thoughts positive and outgoing, it will be easier to go up to someone and introduce yourself. You'll also come across as confident and as somebody that people want to get to know.

Waiting for introductions

Once you've acknowledged that there are acquaintances to be made, don't wait for others to make the first move. "It's a mistake to wait for others to introduce themselves,"

"It's taking a passive approach and it's similar to planting yourself in the chair and being the 'potted plant.' It makes people feel that they have to do all the work." And if you don't get the introduction ball rolling, it's quite possible that, either because of laziness or shyness, no one else will be the first to say "Hi."

Establish eye contact, smile, put your hand out to shake, say hello and introduce yourself. People will be relieved and grateful that you've taken the initiative. Of course, pick your conversational partner wisely.

Getting sidelined

Even if you go to the business party with the appropriate festive attitude, you can undermine it if you don't actively participate. Move towards the area of the room where people are congregating, It shows you are available for conversation and that you're confident and ready to interact. You don't have to be in perpetual motion, but when you do stop, find a spot conducive to communication.

Posturing poorly

When people are tense or bored they tend to slouch and cross their arms. They don't smile, and if they're nervous, they avoid making eye contact. These are the wrong messages to send at a party. It's like putting up a "don't talk to me" sign or worse, one that reads,

Never saying goodbye

People come to parties to mingle. If you hold onto the one person you know at a party as if he or she is a life preserver, you won't seem open and won't meet many people. It's important to get to know others.

A nice gesture is repeating something the person told you and remarking on how you found the comment interesting. If you sincerely want to speak to this person again, ask if you could stay in contact and exchange business cards.

READING

Reading is the most important way to learn English.

Before you can start speaking and writing in English, your brain must get enough input.

There are two ways to get correct English sentences:

— Listening and Reading.

Both are good, but reading is usually much easier than listening. With the help of a good dictionary, you will be able to understand English texts much more easily than, English television or movies.

Reading can really change your English

It can let you use English grammar and vocabulary naturally and fluently.

If you read a few books in English, you will see that your English has become better. You will start using new vocabulary and grammar in your compositions and e-mail messages. You will be surprised, but English phrases will just come to you when you are writing or speaking!

Things like the past simple tense and how to use the word "since" will become part of you. You will use them automatically, without thinking. Correct phrases will just appear in your head. It will be easy to use English, because your brain will only be *repeating the things that it has seen many times*. By reading a book in English, you have given your brain thousands of English sentences.

For example How can you make a mistake and say "I feeled bad", if you have seen the correct phrase ("I felt bad") many times in the last book you've read? You simply cannot make that mistake anymore.

How to read

These great results come especially quickly if you do these things when reading:

1. *Pay attention to interesting things*: new words, phrases, and grammar structures.
2. *Use your dictionary to learn about these interesting things* The more you use your dictionary, the faster your progress. If you don't like to stop reading (to look up a word in your dictionary), you can write down all the interesting sentences, or you can underline them in the book with a pencil. You can learn the words and grammar in these sentences later.

What to read

You should always read English texts which are at the "right level".

There should be some words that you don't know, because you want to learn something. However, there shouldn't be too many difficult words, because you don't want to use your dictionary 10 times in one sentence.

Using better words

adjacent to	Near, next to
Ameliorate	Improve
Amidst	Amid
Amongst	Among
Approximately	About
Ascertain	Learn

Assistance	Help
At an early date	Soon
At present/at the present time	Now
Attempt	Try
Beverage	Drink
Commence	Begin, Start
Concept	Idea
Concerning	About
Construct	Build, make
Converse	Talk
Customary	Usual
Deceased	Dead
Demise	Death
Demonstrate	Show
Dentures	False teeth
Despite	Although
Discontinue	Stop
Dispatch	Send
Donate	Give
Draw to the attention of	Point out
Dwell	Live
Edifice	Building
Endeavor	Try
Eventuate	Happen
Evince	Show
Exceedingly	Very

Expedite	Hurry
Extremely	Very
Facilitate	Ease, help
Finalize	Complete
Following	After
Frequently	Often
Implement	Carry out
in addition	Also
Somewhat	Rather
Subsequently	Later
Sufficient	Enough
Terminate	End
to date	So far
Transportation	Transport
Upon	On
Utilize	Use
Venue	Place
was of the opinion that	Thought
was suffering from	Had
when and if	If
Whilst	While
with the exception of	Except

But anytime you want to use a better word please think:

1. Is it the exact word you need?
2. Is there an alternative that would be as accurate - and more comprehensible?

Words people get wrong

First, here's a list of words that many people can't spell. Get somebody to test you on it.

- Abhorrence
- Accidentally
- Accommodation
- Acquiescence
- Admissible
- Annihilate
- Apartment
- Authoritative
- Auxiliary
- Benefited
- Blamable
- Bureaucracy
- Consensus
- Convertible
- Debatable
- Definitely
- Descendant
- Destructible
- Diagrammatic
- Dissatisfaction
- Ecstasy
- Effervescence
- Eligibility

— Embarrass
— Emissary
— Exaggerate
— Exhilaration
— Expatriate
— Forty
— Fulfilling
— Funereal
— Harass
— Hiccup
— Hierarchy
— Humorous
— Hygiene
— Hysterical
— Ideologist
— Indispensable
— Jeopardize
— Liaison
— Maintenance
— Meanness
— Millennium
— Miniature
— Miscellaneous
— Mischievous
— Noticeable
— Occurred

- Omitted
- Privilege
- Profession
- Proprietary
- Rarefy
- Recommend
- Separate
- Statutory

So, all that you now need to put together is:

- Kill your Fear!
- Practice Grammatically Correct English.
- Make better your vocabulary.
- Understand the art of good conversation.
- Understand the idea of small talk.
- Speak with Confidence.

3

Advanced English

SUBJECTS AND VERBS AGREEMENT

Subjects and Verbs agreement is a must for any sentence.

Verb must agree with its Subject in Number and Person

Often, by what is called the 'Error of Proximity', the verb is made to agree with the subject which is nears to it rather than to its proper Subject.

Example-1:

— The quality of the mangoes were not good.

In this sentence, the verb is 'were' whereas the proper Subject is the quality of the Mangoes. Since 'the quality of the Mangoes' is singular in nature, the singular verb 'was' should have been used in stead of 'were'.

So the correct sentence is:

— The quality of the Mangoes was not good.

Example-2:

— The introduction of coffee and other beverages have not been without some effect.

In this sentence as well, the proper Subject is 'The introduction of ....'. This Subject is singular. So the verb 'has', meant for the singular Subject, should have been used in place of 'have' which is a plural verb.

The correct sentence is:

— The introduction of coffee and other beverages has not been without some effects.

Example-3:

— The results of the recognition is this fact is seen in a gradual manner.

In this sentence, the proper Subject is 'The results of the recognition' which is plural. But the singular verb 'is' has been used in place of 'are'.

So the correct sentence is:

— The results of introduction are seen in a gradual manner.

This sentence is an example for Subject-and-Verb-agreement.

The verb must agree with the Subject when the Subject is the combination of two or more nouns or pronouns joined by 'and'.

Example-1:

— Fire and water does not agree.

In this sentence, the subject is 'Fire and water' which is plural in form. But the sentence uses the verb 'does' which treats only the noun 'water' as the Subject.

So the correct sentence is:

— Fire and water do not agree.

Example-2:

— Honour and glory is the reward.

Here also the Subject is in plural form i.e. Honour and glory.

So the correct form of the sentence is:

— Honour and glory are the rewards.

This sentence is an example for Subject-and-Verb-agreement. Here not only the verb has been changed to make the sentence correct one. But also the corresponding change in the object 'reward' has been made. The object 'reward' has been changed into 'rewards'. But when the two nouns refer to the same person or to the same idea, only the singular form of the verb should be used.

Example-3:

— The novelist and poet are dead.

In this sentence, both the novelist and the poet are one and the same person. In case they are different person, this sentence might have been in the following form:

— The novelist and the poet are dead.

The absence of the article 'the' before the word 'poet' indicates that both the persons are one and the same person.

So the correct sentence is:

— The novelist and poet is dead.

Example-4:

— My friend and benefactor have come.

This sentence is a wrong one.

The correct sentence is:

— My friend and benefactor has come.

This sentence is an example for Subject-and-Verb-agreement.

When the Subject is formed by the conjunctions such as 'with' as well as, along with etc...' the verb should be in singular form.

Example-1:

— The house, with its contents, was insured.

In this sentence, the Subject is only the house, not its contents although the verb 'insure' refers to the contents as well.

Examples:

— Justice, as well as mercy, allows it.

— English, as well as Japanese, is taught there.

— Silver, as well as Cotton, has fallen in price.

These sentence are examples for Subject-and-Verb-agreement.

Two singular Subjects connected by 'or' or 'nor' require a singular verb.

Example-1:

— Our happiness or our sorrow is largely due to our actions.

Here the Subject is either 'our happiness' or 'our sorrow'. So it requires only singular verb.

Example-2:

— Neither food nor water is to be found here.

Here also the Subject is either 'food' or 'water'. So it requires singular verb.

Examples:

— Either the cat or the dog is good for you.

— Either this College or any other college in this country is suitable for you.

Note: When one of the Subjects, joined by 'or' or 'nor', is plural, the verb must be plural. The plural object should be placed near the verb.

Example-1:

— Neither the Chairman nor the members were present.

Here in this sentence, the Subject that the verb takes 'the members' has been placed near the verb 'were'.

Example-2:

— Neither his brother nor his parents were with him.

Her also the same system has been followed.

Examples:

— Neither your father nor your friends are welcome to the function.

— Neither he nor his employees attended the festival

This sentence is an example for Subject-and-Verb-agreement.

The words 'many, neither, many a, each, everyone, every etc..' require only singular verbs.

Example-1:

— Many a students is standing in the canteen

Although the word preceding the verb 'is' is plural in nature, the correct verb is singular one 'is', because of the presence of 'many a'.

Example-2:

— Each of these items is found in Sri Lanka.

Here also the Subject is singular in form 'each of...' So the verb is in singular form. This sentence is an example for Subject-and-Verb-agreement.

Examples:

— Neither of the two men was strong.

— Neither of two brothers was selected to the post.

— Every one of the prisons is full.

These sentences are examples for Subject-and-Verb-agreement.

When the Subjects, joined by 'or' or 'nor', the verb agrees with the Subject which is near to the verb.

Example-1:

— Either you or I am mistaken

Here the Subject that the verb takes is the pronoun 'I'. The same sentence can be rewritten as:

— Either I or you are mistaken.

Although, this sentence is grammatically correct, the previous sentence is preferred to this one. Because, when we use many pronouns in a sentence, we have to use them in the order: Third person, second person and the first person. Such a usage constitutes Perfect English.

Examples:

— Neither he nor you are a member of this organisation.

— Either you or I am to blame.

— Neither he nor they have agreed to help me.

— Either You or he has consulted me.

These sentences are examples for Subject-and-Verb-agreement. have seen how the Subject and Verb agreement in a sentence is must.

Two nouns qualified by 'each' or 'every', even though connected by and, require only a singular verb.

Example-1:

— Every boy and every girl is given the admission ticket to the show.

In this sentence, the Subject is 'Every boy and every girl'. Although this Subject contains two nouns and they are connected by the conjunction 'and', we have to use only a singular verb 'is', because the subject implies every one of all the students.

Example-2:

— Every man and every woman was given a packet of sweets.

In this sentence also, the Subject is treated as singular, so the verb is also singular. You see how in this sentence Subject-and-Verb-agreement is perfect.

Examples:

- Every teacher and every student has got his share of the balance amount.
- Every boy and every girl in this class has applied for TOEFL.
- Every man and every woman has come forward to donate some money to this organisation.

Few nouns which are plural in form but singular in meaning take only the singular verb.

Examples:

- The news is not true.
- The wages of sin is pains.
- Mathematics is a branch of study in every school.
- Economics is a scientific subject.

You see how in these sentences Subject-and-Verb-agreement is perfect.

The Subjects 'pains' and 'means' take either singular or plural verb. But the construction should be onsistent.

Examples:

- Great pains have been taken to complete this project.
- Great pains has been taken to complete this project.

Both these sentences are correct forms but when you use a particular form, you have to use that form consistently throughout the particular writing.

— The means to rich is a not a secret.

— The means to rich are not secrets.

When a plural noun denotes a specific quantity or amount considered as a whole, the verb is generally singular.

Examples:

— Fifteen minutes is not sufficient.

— Ten kilometers is a long distance.

— Fifty thousands dollars is not a small salary per month.

— Three parts of the project is left to me.

The Verb in the Subordinate Clause:

Example-1:

— India is one of the few countries which have their own traditions.

Do you think this sentence is a correct one? The Subordinate Clause in this sentence takes plural verb while the Main Clause takes only a singular verb. Because the Subject of the Subordinate Clause 'which' here means only the word 'countries' which comes before it. So, the Subordinate Clause takes a plural verb. This sentence is correct one.

Examples:

— Is you brother one of the two hundred people who have become the members of this organisation?

- This is one of those novels that deal with drug abuse.
- Ramanujam is one of the greatest mathematicians who have ever lived.
- The neighbour, with his wife and children, is watching the football match on television.
- Neither my bank balance nor the amount I borrowed is sufficient to meet the expenditure.
- Not one in hundred seeds develops into a healthy plant.
- The number of poisonous snakes in not known.
- A good college record as well a good score in GMAT is required for admission in MBA.
- Not only an excellent preparation but also very good presentation in TOEFL is must to score more marks in it.
- Neither of these two movies was rated as outstanding, but each had an absorbing story.
- A large percentage of college students were absent on the annual day.

PROPER USE OF TENSES

Let us see how the tenses should be used in various sentences.

If the action was started in the Past and is continuing still now, You should use the present perfect continuous tense, and not the present continuous tense.

Example-1:

- He is working in this office for the last five years.

Here, in this sentence, it has been stated that he started working in the office five years back and he still works there. So the correct tense to be used is not the present continuous tense, but the past perfect continuous tense.

The correct answer is:

— He has been working in this office for the last five years.

Example-2:

— Mary is living in New York for the last seven months.

This also has the same mistake.

The correct tense is:

— Mary has been living in New York for the last seven months.

Examples:

— Mr. Clinton has been working as the Chairman of this Company for the last two years.

— She has been working as a Professor of Chemistry for the last twenty five years.

— It has been living with me for the last three months only.

If an action had happened at a particular point of time in the past, you should use only the simple past tense, not the present perfect tense or past perfect tense.

Examples:

— Incorrect: My mother had visited the Niagara Falls last year. My mother has visited the Niagara Falls last year.

- Correct: My mother visited the Niagara Falls.
- Incorrect: Philip's father has died last month. Philip's father had died last year.
- Correct: Philip's father died last year.

When the main clause is in the simple future tense, the subordinate clause should not be in the future tense but should be in simple present tense.

Examples:

- Incorrect: When I shall find out Clinton's address, I shall tell you.
- Correct: When I find out Clinton's address, I shall tell you.
- Incorrect: Nita will start crying, if we will tease her.
- Correct: Nita will start crying, if we tease her.
- Incorrect: As soon as we will receive your order with payment, we shall ship the goods to you.
- Correct: As soon as we receive your order with payment, we shall ship the goods to you.

In the sentences in the subjunctive mood (containing a command, an order, a suggestion, a warning or a request), You should not use the future tense in the subordinate clause, but use simple present tense.

Examples:

- Incorrect: Take care that you should not trip over the carpet.
- Correct: Take care that you do not trip over the carpet.

— Incorrect: Please ensure that you will not be late for the meeting.

— Correct: Please ensure that you are not late for the meeting.

— Incorrect: We expect that the bill will be paid very soon.

— Correct: WE expect that the bill is paid very soon.

In a sentence mentioning two mutually related past events of which one had happened earlier than the other, they should not both be mentioned in the simple past tense. The earlier event must be mentioned in the past perfect tense and the later event must be mentioned in the simple past tense.

Examples:

— Incorrect: The bus already left by the time I reached the station.

— Correct. The bus already had left by the time I reached the station.

— Incorrect: Before I bought this house last month, I lived in it as a tenant for three years.

— Correct: Before I bought this house last month, I had lived in it as a tenant for three years.

— Incorrect: The teacher complained to the headmaster that the students misbehaved in the class.

— Correct: The teacher complained to the headmaster that the students had misbehaved in the class.

— Incorrect: He left the hotel before I reached it.

— Correct: He had left the hotel before I reached it.

When the main clause is in the past tense, the subordinate clause can be either in the past tense or in the past perfect tense. It can not be in any of the present or future tense forms.

Examples:

— Incorrect: Clinton told me that he will come to the office tomorrow.

— Correct: Clinton told me that he would come to the office tomorrow.

— Incorrect: Did you tell me that you have visited Taj Mahal?

— Correct: Did you tell me that you had visited Taj Mahal?

— Incorrect: The accused asserted the Judge that he is innocent.

— Correct: The accused asserted the Judge that he was innocent.

— Incorrect: The students told us that they will take their examinations without fail.

— Correct: The students told us that they would take their examinations without fail.

Exceptions:

When the subordinate clause mentions an eternal truth (namely, a statement that is forever true), it should be in simple present tense even the main clause is in past tense.

Examples:

- The teacher said that the Sun rises in the east.
- Columbus proved that the Earth is round.
- Newton discovered that it is the gravitational force that keeps the planets moving round the Sun.

PARALLELISM

Parallelism is a balance in the structure of the sentence. Look at the following sentence.

- Air travel is safe, fast and it is convenient.

In this sentence, three attributes of air travel are sought to be enumerated in this sentence. Of these, the first two are mentioned a single words (safe and fast), while the third is mentioned as an independent main clause. (It is convenient) This sentence lacks parallelism in structure which is considered a grammatical error.

The correct form is:

- Air travel is safe, fast and convenient.

Lack of parallelism may arise in many different ways.

Example-1:

- Swimming, seeing movies and to go for walk are my hobbies.

In this sentence also the first two hobbies (swimming and seeing movies) have been given in single words while third hobby (to go for walk) has been mentioned in an infinite form. This sentence lacks the parallelism.

The correct sentence is:

— Swimming, seeing movies and walking are my hobbies.

Example-2:

— We should vote for Clinton because he is honest, knowledgeable and he is a hard-working.

This sentence also states three qualities about Clinton. But the first tow qualities have been stated as adjectives whereas the third quality has been noted in a subordinate clause. In order to restore the parallelism, this sentence should be rearranged as follows.

— We should vote for Clinton because he is honest, knowledgeable and hard-working.

Example-3:

Incorrect:

— The board decided to pass the bill, approve the contract and it would reelect the Chairman.

Correct:

— The board decided to pass the bill, approve the contract and reelect the Chairman.

Example-4:

Incorrect:

— Every night, I go for a walk, wash my teeth and would read a book before going to my bed.

Correct:

— Every night, I go for a walk, wash my teeth and read a book before going to my bed.

Example-5:

Incorrect:

— The museum contains sixth century sculptures, eighteenth century swords and the dress worn by nineteenth century royal family.

Correct:

— The museum contains sixth century sculptures, eighteenth century swords and nineteenth century royal dress.

Example-6:

Incorrect:

— Europe's travel industry is suffering as a result of a sluggish economy, a stretch of bad weather, as well as the chilling effects of terrorist activity that is persistent.

Correct:

— Europe's travel industry is suffering as a result of a sluggish economy, a stretch of bad weather And the chilling effects of persistent terrorist activity.

Example-7:

Incorrect:

— The suspect in the burglary was advised of his right to remain silent, told he could not leave, and was interrogated in a detention room.

Correct:

— The suspect in the burglary was advised of his right to remain silent, told he could not leave, and interrogated in a detention room.

These examples might have given you better ideas about the ways to restore the parallelism in a sentence.

SYMMETRY

Symmetry between the two parts of a sentence is must.

Look at this sentence.

— To advance was difficult: retreating was impossible.

Here, in the first part of the sentence, an infinite has been used. While in the second part of the sentence only a gerund has been used. This sentence does not have symmetry. In order to restore that, this sentence should be restructured as follows.

— To advance was difficult: to retreat was impossible.

Or this sentence can be written in another form.

— Advancing was difficult; retreating was impossible.

Example-1:

— To visualise success is not the same as achieving it.

There is no symmetry in this sentence.

The correct forms are:

— To visualise success is not the same as to achieve it.

— Visualising success is not the same as achieving it.

Example-2:

Incorrect:

— To say that the songs patterns of the common robin are less complex than those of the indigo bunting is doing a great disservice to both birds.

Correct:

— To say that the songs patterns of the common robin are less complex than those of the indigo bunting is to do a great disservice to both birds.

Example-3:

Incorrect:

— I spent three weeks in France, and my images of that country range from pastoral to the cosmopolitan.

Correct:

— I spent three weeks in France, and my images of that country range from the pastoral to the cosmopolitan.

Example-4:

Incorrect:

— In the Chinese restaurant in our town, the food is fascinating and the liquor exquisite.

Correct:

— In the Chinese restaurant in our town, the food is fascinating and the liquor is exquisite.

Example-5:

Incorrect:

— Because young children do not organise their

attention or perceptions systematically like adults, they may notice and remember details that their elders ignore.

Correct:

— Because young children do not organise their attention or perceptions systematically as adults do, they may notice and remember details that their elders ignore.

Note: The word 'like' is only a preposition. It is not a conjunction. The proper conjunction is only 'as'.

Example-6:

Incorrect:

— There is growing demand in the state for initiative and referendum, a procedure that allows the voters to propose laws as well as repealing them.

Correct:

— There is growing demand in the state for initiative and referendum, a procedure that allows the voters to propose laws as well as to repeal them.

PRONOUNS

A Pronouns is word that is used in place of another noun in order to avoid inelegant repetition.

Example:

— Clinton said that Clinton was planning to go with Clinton's brother to Clinton's school.

This sentence is, although grammatically correct one, not preferred and is looking awkward. In order to avoid the inelegant repetition of the same word (Noun-Clinton), 'he' and 'his' can be used as follows.

— Clinton said that he was planning to go with his brother to his school.

By using 'he' and 'his', we have made the sentences an elegant one. Singular Pronouns: I, you, he, she, it, each, everyone, one, me, him, his, her, this etc... Plural Pronouns: They, both, few, those, these etc... Pronouns which could be either singular or plural: Who, which, what, that etc... The noun that a pronoun stands for is known as antecedent.

Example:

— Joseph has gone to meet his friend.

In this sentence, the noun 'Joseph' is the antecedent for 'his'. The following rules must be strictly observed.

A Pronoun must be of its same number as its antecedent

Example-1:

— A student who aims to get the first rank must invest a significant amount of their time and energy in hard work.

In this sentence, the word 'their' has been used whereas there is no antecedent for that in the sentence. This sentence uses only a singular noun 'a student'. So the proper word that should be used to denote the singular noun is only 'his' or 'her'.

The correct sentence is:

— A student who aims to get the first rank must invest a significant amount of his time and energy in hard work.

Example-2:

— Unlike their counterparts in other Western Countries, The American labor movement has never embraced revolutionary ideologies for the ultimate transformation of the economic order.

In this sentence, the pronoun 'theirs' has been used without any antecedent. But the following sentence uses a singular noun 'the American labor movement'. So the proper word to be used here is only 'its'.

The correct sentence is:

— Unlike its counterparts in other Western Countries, The American labor movement has never embraced revolutionary ideologies for the ultimate transformation of the economic order.

A Pronoun must be of the same gender as its antecedent:

Example-1:

— The batting team in cricket has eleven players, of which two will be at the crease at any moment.

In this sentence, the pronoun 'which' has been used whereas the Noun speaks about only players. For this Noun, the word to be used is only 'whom'.

The correct sentence is:

— The batting team in cricket has eleven players, of whom two will be at the crease at any moment.

Example-2:

— This university has twenty thousands students of which only a few hundreds belong to this state.

This sentence also has the same mistake which the previous one has.

The correct sentence is:

— This university has twenty thousands students of whom only a few hundreds belong to this state.

There must be no ambiguity regarding the antecedent of a pronoun:

Example-1:

— John asked Clinton to bring his cricket bat.

In this sentence, the word 'his' has been used. But it is not clear whose cricket-bat this sentence is talking about. There is ambiguity in the uses of the pronoun. In order to make the sentence unambiguous one, it is better to use the same noun.

The correct sentence is:

— John asked Clinton to bring Clinton's cricket bat.

Example-2:

— My friend requested his father to tell his mother about his success in the university exams.

Here this sentence has the same mistake as the previous one.

The correct sentence is:

— My friend requested his father to tell his father's mother about his success in the university exams.

A pronoun should not be used without an antecedent noun to it:

Example:

- I have studied well for TOEFL and it has given me the confidence that I will score more than 90%.

This sentence uses the word 'it' whereas there is no antecedent to that pronoun in the sentence.

The correct sentence is:

- The fact that I have studied well for TOEFL has given me confidence that I will score more than 90%.

There must be consistency in the use of indefinite pronoun 'one' in a sentence:

Example-1:

- If one looks at the clear sky away from the glare of the city, he can see not less that 3000 stars with his naked eyes.

In this sentence, the words 'he' and 'his' have been used whereas in the first part of the sentence the indefinite pronoun 'one' has been used. This kind of inconsistency in the uses of indefinite pronoun 'one' will spoil the beauty of the sentence.

The correct sentence is:

- If one looks at the clear sky away from the glare of the city, one can see not less that 3000 stars with one's naked eyes.
- If he looks at the clear sky away from the glare of the city, he can see not less that 3000 stars with his naked eyes.

Both these sentences are the correct forms.

Examples:

Incorrect:

— More than five thousand years ago, Chinese scholars accurately described the flow of blood as a continuous circle controlled by the heart. But it went unnoticed in the West.

Correct:

— More than five thousand years ago, Chinese scholars accurately described the flow of blood as a continuous circle controlled by the heart. But the discovery went unnoticed in the West.

Incorrect:

— India is a country with at least fifty major regional languages, of whom fourteen have official recognition.

Correct:

— India is a country with at least fifty major regional languages, of which fourteen have official recognition.

PREPOSITIONS

Nouns, verbs, adjectives and participles are often combined with Prepositions. Each such combination has a separate meaning, sometimes totally different from the main word. Such a preposition, in combination with a noun or a verb or an adjective or a participle is called Prepositional Phrase. Here are few examples of sentences with such Prepositional Phrases. Such Prepositional Phrases are called IDIOMS. The idioms have fixed meanings.

Examples:

— Every citizen should abide by the laws of his country.

— This lake abounds in fish.

— Rajeev Gandhi started his Prime Ministership with an abundance of goodwill from Indians.

— Why were you absent from the class yesterday?

— When I entered the room, I found my father absorbed in deep thought.

— The Judge refused to accede to the request of the accused to release him on bail.

— I regret that your proposal is acceptable to me.

— Gupta is known to all the politicians, and has ready access to a number of ministers.

— The engineer was accused of taking a bribe from the contractor.

— Are you acquainted with this neighbourhood?

— The accused was acquitted of the charges of perjury.

— You have to adopt yourself to the changing times.

Note: Quite often, as in the previous case and in the following case, the main word and the preposition may be separated by other intervening words.

— I was dissuaded by my uncle from applying for that job.

— I was not aware of your presence at the meeting.

— Do you expect the teacher to be fair in awarding marks for the essays?

Phrasal verb is formed by combining a verb with a preposition.

Examples:

- The boy, who pleaded guilty to stealing the pen, was admonished by the Judge.
- Cunning is the quality that is popularly attributed to the fox.
- Known to be highly irritable, my uncle is avoided by all the children.
- Small pox vaccine is produced by introducing the virus into the bloodstream of a horse.

The word consider:

The word consider should be used without preposition following it. The uses of the phrases 'consider as', 'consider to be' and 'consider as being' are wrong.

Example:

- Mahatma Gandhi is considered as one of the greatest Indians.

This sentence is wrong one. The correct sentence is:

- Mahatma Gandhi is considered one of the greatest Indians.

The word regard:

The correct phrase involving 'regard' is 'regard as'. The phrases 'regarding to be' and 'regarding as being' are wrong ones.

Example:

— The writer Alice Walker regards Steve Wonder to be a spiritual singer rather than a pop singer.

This is an incorrect sentence. The correct sentence is:

— The writer Alice Walker regards Steve Wonder as a spiritual singer rather than as a pop singer.

Examples:

— This advertisement is aimed at teenagers.

— This columnist was accurate in predicting the outcome of the elections.

Now let us see how the idioms are used in the sentences. Many verbs when followed by various prepositions or adverbs acquire the idiomatic expressions.

Examples:

— He seems to be well off. (In comfortable position)

— That fellow trumped up a story. (Fabricated)

— He is sticking out for better terms. (Persisting in demanding)

— I threatened to show him up. (Expose)

— During her long illness, she often longed for health. (Desired)

— About an hour ago, I saw a fellow hanging about our bungalow. (Loitering about)

— Rust has eaten away the iron. (Corroded)

Many such Prepositional Phrases get their figurative meanings which are quite different from eh meanings of the main words.

MODIFIERS

In many sentences, the Modifiers might have been misplaced. They should be placed properly so as the make the sentences correct ones. As we have seen already, the Adjective and the Adverb are modifying the sentences. So they are called so. An Adjective is the word that gives some additional information about the noun. An Adverb is the word that gives some additional information about the verb or an adjective or another adverb. Both these adjective and adverb are called the modifiers. An adjective need not be a single word, but can be phrase consisting of many words or can even be a full subordinate clause with its own subject and predicate.

Adjectival Modifiers:

The modifiers of adjective are called the Adjectival Modifiers.

Examples:

- A number of applications received for the jobs.
- Puny and silent, George generally goes unnoticed in any group.
- The stem in the part of the brain that connects the cerebral cortex to the spinal cord

Adverbial Modifiers:

The modifiers of adverbs are called the Adverbial Modifiers.

Examples:

- Do not walk that fast. I could not keep face with you.

— A Member of the Parliament should not vote in the house before he takes the oath of allegation to the Constitution.

These modifiers, in few sentences, might have been misplaced. We have to set it right to see that the sentence goes right.

Example-1:

— Having apologized for the misbehaviour, the teacher permitted the student to reenter the class room.

As per this sentence, it is only the teacher who misbehaved. Who apologized to whom? Did the student apologized to the teacher or the teacher apologized to the student in the class? But the author of this sentence indented to say that after the student, who misbehaved, apologized, And then the teacher permitted them to reenter the class room. In this case, this given sentence should be corrected as.

— Having apologized for misbehaviour, the student was permitted by the teacher to reenter the class room.

Note: The participle should be used for the subject for which is intended.

Example-2:

— Attempting to smuggle Gold, the customs officials detained the passenger.

Who attempted to smuggle Gold? The customs officials or the Passenger? Certainly, it is only the passenger who might have attempted to smuggle Gold. So this given sentence should be corrected as:

— Attempting to smuggle Gold, the passenger was detained by the customs officials.

Example-3:

— Walking along the edge of the lake, the fish suddenly jumped out and fell near me.

Who walked along the edge of the lake? Is it the fish? Certainly no So this sentence should be corrected as.

— Walking along the edge of the lake, I found that a fish suddenly jumped out and fell near me.

Example-4:

— Having paid the fine, the police-officer allowed the car-driver to go.

Who paid the fine? The police-officer or the car-driver... Certainly it only the car-driver... This sentence should be corrected as:

— Having paid the fine, the car-driver was allowed by the police-officer to go.

Example-5:

Possessing fifteen legs, I have never seen such a creature in my life. Who is possessing fifteen legs? Is it I or the creature? Certainly it is only the creature. So the correct sentence is:

— Possessing fifteen legs, this creature is never seen by me in my life.

Few more examples have been given here with the correct version for your kind attention.

1. Frail and weak, the heavy cart could not be

drawn over the gradient by the bullock. (Incorrect)

Frail and weak, the bullock could not draw the heavy cart over the gradient. (Correct)

2. Banned in India, I could not bring the book 'Satanic Verses' into the country. (Incorrect)

   Banned in India, The book 'Satanic Verses' could not be brought to the country by me. (Correct)

3. Delightfully cooked by his father, Clinton loves peas. (Incorrect)

   Delightfully cooked by his father, the peas were loved by Clinton. (Correct)

4. Though faded because of rough use, she wore the red-sari for the function. (Incorrect)

   Though faded because of rough use, the red-sari was worn by her for the function. (Correct)

5. Dug out from fifty feet below the ground, the archaeologist determined the age of the pottery as over thousand years. (Incorrect)

   Dug out from fifty feet below the ground, the potter was determined by the archaeologist as a thousand-year old one. (Correct)

6. After paying for the books, the salesman gave me a calendar as a free compliment. (Incorrect)

   After paying for the books, I was given a calendar by the salesman as a free compliment. (Correct)

7. Even after being dead for 150 yeas, many people still admire the music of Beethoven. (Incorrect)

Even after being dead for 150 yeas, still Beethoven was admired for his music by many people. (Correct)

8. After taking my seat in the plane, the air-hostess offered me chocolates. (Incorrect)

   After taking my seat in the plane, I was offered chocolates by the air-hostess. (Correct)

9. By installing small electric pumps, farmers' houses could be heated by warmth from cows' milk, according to one agricultural engineer. (Incorrect)

   By installing small electric pumps, farmers, according to one agricultural engineer, could use the warmth from cows' milk to heat their houses. (Correct)

10. Coming late to the office for the third time in a week, the manager cut the peon's salary for a day. (Incorrect)

    Coming late to the office for the third time in a week, the peon had his salary for a day cut by the manager. (Correct)

DANGLING MODIFIERS

A Dangling Modifier is a close relative of misplaced modifier. In a sentence involving dangling modifier, the noun which the phrase really modifies will be missing, we ourselves have to supply an appropriate noun with reference to the context.

Example-1:

– Before shifting the hospitals from the present location, the public must be consulted.

In this sentence, it is not clear who is shifting the hospitals. So the adjective 'before shifting the hospitals' is dangling without an appropriate noun for it.

The correct sentence is:

— Before shifting the hospitals from the present location, the officials should consult the public.

So is only the officials who will shift the hospitals therefore it is only they who should consult the public.

Example-2:

— Using the Doppler ultrasound device, fatal heartbeats can be detected by the twelfth week of pregnancy.

In this sentence also, it is not clear who is using the Doppler ultrasound device? So the correct sentence is:

— Using the Doppler ultrasound device, the doctors can detect fatal heartbeats by the twelfth week of pregnancy.

A sentence without a misplaced modifier and a dangling modifier will always add beauty.

4

Use of Idioms and Phrases

Idiom may be defined as expression peculiar to a language. It plays an important part in all languages. Many verbs, when followed by various prepositions, or by adverbs, acquire an idiomatic sense.

Example-1:

— He backed up his friends' claim.

In this sentence, the verb 'back' has been paired with the preposition 'up' and is giving the meaning 'supporting'. Whereas the verb 'back' means another meaning.

— He supported his friends' claim.

This kind of expression is called Idiomatic expression.

Examples:

In few of the following these sentences the idioms are coloured blue and their meanings are given in the bracket.

— The present disturbances will soon blow over. (Pass off)

— The police produced the evidences to bear out the charge of murder. (Substantiate)

- You must not build your hopes upon his promises. (Rely upon)
- The matter has been cleared up. (Explained)
- I readily closed with his offer. (Accepted)
- He is ready to dispose off his car. (Sell)
- Rust has eaten away the plate. (Corroded)
- They fixed upon him to do the work. (Chose)
- My good behaviour so far gained on my father. (Won the favour of)
- Please hear me out. (Hear me to the end)

Note: As in the previous sentence, few other words may be used between the two parts of the idioms. Now, let us see how few verbs get their idiomatic formations when they are paired with the prepositions.

Key-Word based idioms have been listed below.

A chain is no stronger than its weakest link: This means that processes, organisations, etc, are vulnerable because the weakest person or part can always damage or break them.

- *A little learning is a dangerous thing:* A small amount of knowledge can cause people to think they are more expert than they really are. eg. he said he'd done a course on home electrics, but when he tried to mend my table lamp, he fused all the lights! I think a little learning is a dangerous thing
- *A long row to hoe:* Something that is a long row to hoe is a difficult task that takes a long time.

- *A lost ball in the high weeds:* A lost ball in the high weeds is someone who does not know what they are doing, where they are or how to do something.
- *A penny for your thoughts:* This idiom is used as a way of asking someone what they are thinking about.
- *A penny saved is a penny earned:* This means that we shouldn't spend or waste money, but try to save it.
- *A picture is worth a thousand words:* A picture can often get a message across much better than the best verbal description.
- *A poor man's something:* Something or someone that can be compared to something or someone else, but is not as good is a poor man's version; a writer who uses lots of puns but isn't very funny would be a poor man's Oscar Wilde.
- *A watched pot never boils:* Some things work out in their own time, so being impatient and constantly checking will just make things seem longer.
- *Abide by a decision:* If you abide by a decision, you accept it and comply with it, even though you might disagree with it.
- *Abject lesson:* (India) An abject lesson serves as a warning to others.
- *About as useful as a chocolate teapot:* Someone or something that is of no practical use is about as useful as a chocolate teapot.

- *About face:* If someone changes their mind completely, this is an about face. It can be used when companies, governments, etc, change their position on an issue.
- *Ace up your sleeve:* If you have an ace up your sleeve, you have something that will give you an advantage that other people don't know about.
- *Babe in arms:* A babe in arms is a very young child, or a person who is very young to be holding a position.
- *Babe in the woods:* A babe in the woods is a naive, defenceless, young person.
- *Baby boomer:* (USA) A baby boomer is someone born in the years after the end of the Second World War, a period when the population was growing very fast.
- *Back burner:* If an issue is on the back burner, it is being given low priority.
- *Back foot:* (UK) If you are on your back foot, you are at a disadvantage and forced to be defensive of your position.
- *Back number:* Something that's a back number is dated or out of fashion.
- *Back the wrong horse:* If you back the wrong horse, you give your support to the losing side in something.
- *Back to back:* If things happen back to back, they are directly one after another.
- *Back to square one:* If you are back to square one, you have to start from the beginning again.

- *Back to the drawing board*: If you have to go back to the drawing board, you have to go back to the beginning and start something again.
- *Back to the salt mine:* If someone says they have to go back to the salt mine, they have to return to work.
- *Back to the wall:* If you have your back to the wall, you are in a difficult situation with very little room for manoeuvre.
- *Backseat driver:* A backseat driver is an annoying person who is fond of giving advice to the person performing a task or doing something, especially when the advice is either wrong or unwelcome.
- *Bag of bones:* If someone is a bag of bones, they are very underweight.
- *Bag of nerves:* If someone is a bag of nerves, they are very worried or nervous.
- *Ballpark figure:* A ballpark figure is a rough or approximate number (guesstimate) to give a general idea of something, like a rough estimate for a cost, etc.
- *Banana republic:* Banana republic is a term used for small countries that are dependent on a single crop or resource and governed badly by a corrupt elite.
- *Bandit territory:* An area or an industry, profession, etc, where rules and laws are ignored or flouted is bandit territory.
- *Baptism of fire:* A baptism of fire was a soldier's first experience of shooting. Any unpleasant

experience undergone, usually where it is also a learning experience, is a baptism of fire.

- *Bar fly:* A bar fly is a person who spends a lot of time drinking in different bars and pubs.
- *Bark is worse than their bite:* Someone who's bark is worse than their bite may well get angry and shout, but doesn't take action.
- *Barking up the wrong tree:* If you are barking up the wrong tree, it means that you have completely misunderstood something or are totally wrong.
- *Barkus is willing:* This idiom means that someone is willing to get married.
- *Barrack-room lawyer:* (UK) A barrack-room lawyer is a person who gives opinions on things they are not qualified to speak about.
- *Barrel of laughs:* If someone's a barrel of laughs, they are always joking and you find them funny.
- *Basket case:* If something is a basket case, it is so bad that it cannot be helped.
- *Bat an eyelid:* If someone doesn't bat an eyelid, they don't react or show any emotion when surprised, shocked, etc.
- *Batten down the hatches:* If you batten down the hatches, you prepare for the worst that could happen to you.
- *Be all ears:* If you are all ears, you are very eager to hear what someone has to say.
- *Cake's not worth the candle:* If someone says that the cake's not worth the candle, they mean that

the result will not be worth the effort put in to achieve it.

- *Calf lick:* A calf lick is the weird parting in your fringe where your hair grows in a different direction, usually to one side.
- *Call a spade a spade:* A person who calls a spade a spade is one speaks frankly and makes little or no attempt to conceal their opinions or to spare the feelings of their audience.
- *Call it a day:* If you call it a day, you stop doing something for a while, normally at least until the following day.
- *Call on the carpet:* If you are called on the carpet, you are summoned for a reprimand by superiors or others in power.
- *Calm before the storm:* A calm time immediately before period of violent activity or argument is the calm before the storm.
- *Can of worms:* If an action can create serious problems, it is opening a can of worms.
- *Can't do it for toffee*: If you can't so something for toffee, you are incapable of doing something properly or to any sort of standard.
- *Can't hold a candle*: If something can't hold a candle to something else, it is much worse.
- *Card up your sleeve*: If you have a card up your sleeve, you have a surprise plan or idea that you are keeping back until the time is right.
- *Carpetbagger:* A carpetbagger is an opportunist without any scruples or ethics, or a politican

who wants to represent a place they have no connection with.

- *Carry the can:* If you carry the can, you take the blame for something, even though you didn't do it or are only partly at fault.
- *Case by case:* If things are done case by case, each situation or issue is handled separately on its own merits and demerits.
- *Cash in your chips:* If you cash in your chips, you sell something to get what profit you can because you think its value is going to fall. It can also mean 'to die'.
- *Cast aspersion:* If you cast aspersion, you try to blacken someone's name and make people think badly of them.
- *Cast doubt on:* If you make other people not sure about a matter, then you have cast doubt on it.
- *Cast iron stomach:* A person with a cast iron stomach can eat or drink anything without any ill effects.
- *Cast sheep's eyes at:* If you cast sheep's eyes at at someone, you look lovingly or with longing at them.
- *Cast your mind back:* If somebody tells you to cast your mind back on something, they want you to think about something that happened in the past, but which you might not remember very well, and to try to remember as much as possible.
- *Daft as a brush*: (UK) Someone who is daft as a brush is rather stupid.

— *Damp squib*: (UK) If something is expected to have a great effect or impact but doesn't, it is a damp squib.

— *Dancing on someone's grave*: If you will dance on someone's grave, you will outlive or outlast them and will celebrate their demise.

— *Dark horse*: If someone is a dark horse, they are a bit of a mystery.

— *Davey Jones' locker*: Davey Jones' locker is the bottom of the sea or resting place of drowned sailors.

— *Day in the sun*: If you have your day in the sun, you get attention and are appreciated.

— *Daylight robbery*: If you are overcharged or underpaid, it is a daylight robbery; open, unfair and hard to prevent. Rip-off has a similar meaning.

— *Days are numbered*: When someone's days are numbered, they are expected to die soon.

— *Dead air*: When there is a period of total silence, there is dead air.

— *Dead and buried*: If something is dead and buried, it has all long been settled and is not going to be reconsidered.

— *Dead as a dodo*: If something's dead as a dodo, it is lifeless and dull. The dodo was a bird that lived the island of Mauritius. It couldn't fly and was hunted to extinction.

— *Dead as a doornail*: This is used to indicate that something is lifeless.

- *Dead duck*: If something is a dead duck, it is a failure.
- *Dead even*: If people competing are dead even, they are at exactly the same stage or moving at exactly the same speed.
- *Dead from the neck up*: Someone who's dead from the neck up is very stupid indeed.
- *Dead heat*: If a race ends in a dead heat, two or more finish with exactly the same result.
- *Dead heat*: If people finish a race or competition at axactly the same time and it is impossible to declare one of them the winner, it's a dead heat.
- *Dead in the water*: If something is dead in the water, it isn't going anywhere or making any progress.
- *Dead level best*: If you try your dead level best, you try as hard as you possibly could to do something.
- *Dead man walking*: A dead man walking is someone who is in great trouble and will certainly get punished, lose their job or position, etc, soon.
- *Dead meat*: This is used as a way of threatening someone: You'll be dead meat if you don't go along.
- *Dead men's shoes*: If promotion or success requires replacing somebody, then it can only be reached by dead men's shoes' by getting rid of them.
- *Dear John letter*: A letter written by a partner

explaining why they are ending the relationship is a Dear John letter.

- *Each to their own*: Different people have different preferences. In American English, 'Each to his own' is more common.
- *Eager beaver*: A person who is extremely keen is an eager beaver.
- *Eagle eyes*: Someone who has eagle eyes sees everything; no detail is too small.
- *Early bath*: (UK) If someone has or goes for an early bath, they quit or lose their job or position earlier than expected because things have gone wrong.
- *Early bird catches the worm*: The early bird catches the worm means that if you start something early, you stand a better chance of success.
- *Early to bed, early to rise, makes a man healthy wealthy and wise*: It means that sleeping well and not staying up late will help you out physically and financially.
- *Earn a living*: To make money Ex: We need to get a good job to earn a decent living.
- *Easier said than done*: If something is easier said than done, it is much more difficult than it sounds. It is often used when someone advises you to do something difficult and tries to make it sound easy.
- *Easy as ABC*: Something that is as easy as ABC is very easy or simple.
- *Easy as beans*: Something that is so easy that anyone can do it is easy as beans.

- *Easy as pie*: If something is easy as pie, it is very easy indeed.
- *Easy come, easy go*: This idiom means that money or other material gains that come without much effort tend to get spent or consumed as easily.
- *Easy peasy*: (UK) If something is easy peasy, it is very easy indeed.
- *Eat crow*: (USA) If you eat crow, you have to admit that you were wrong about something.
- *Eat humble pie*: If someone apologises and shows a lot of contrition for something they have done, they eat humble pie.
- *Eat like a bird*: If someone eats like a bird, they eat very little.
- *Eat like a horse*: Someone who eats like a horse, eats a lot.
- *Eat like a pig*: If some eats like a pig, they either eat too much or they have bad table manners.
- *Eat my hat*: People say this when they don't believe that something is going to happen e.g. 'If he passes that exam, I'll eat my hat!'
- *Eat someone alive*: If you eat someone alive, you defeat or beat them comprehensively.
- *Eat your heart out*: If someone tells you to eat your heart out, they are saying they are better than you at something.
- *Eat your words*: If you eat your words, you accept publicly that you were wrong about something you said.
- *Economical with the truth*: (UK) If someone, especially a politician, is economical with the

truth, they leave out information in order to create a false picture of a situation, without actually lying.

- *Egg on your face*: If someone has egg on their face, they are made to look foolish or embarrassed.
- *Elbow grease*: If something requires elbow grease, it involves a lot of hard physical work.
- *Elbow room*: If you haven't got enough elbow room, you haven't got enough space.
- *Elephant in the room*: An elephant in the room is a problem that everyone knows very well but no one talks about because it is taboo, embarrassing, etc.
- *Eleventh hour*: If something happens at the eleventh hour, it happens right at the last minute.
- *Empty vessels make the most noise*: The thoughtless often speak the most.
- *End in smoke*: If something ends in smoke, it produces no concrete or positive result. This expression refers to the boasting by a person, of having put in a lot of efforts by him, for a particular cause or to attain a result which is very difficult to be done by any person.
- *Even a blind squirrel finds a nut once in a while*: This expression means that even if people are ineffective or misguided, sometimes they can still be correct just by being lucky.
- *Even a broken clock is right twice a day*: This is used when people get lucky and are undeservedly successful.

— *Face like thunder*: If someone has a face like thunder, they are clearly very angry or upset about something.

— *Face only a mother could love*: When someone has a face only a mother could love, they are ugly.

— *Face the music*: If you have to face the music, you have to accept the negative consequences of something you have done wrong.

— *Face value*: If you take something at face value, you accept the appearance rather than looking deeper into the matter.

— *Face your demons*: If you face your demons, you confront your fears or something that you have been trying hard to avoid.

— *Facts of life*: When someone is taught the facts of life, they learn about sex and reproduction.

— *Failure is the mother of success*: Failure is often a stepping stone towards success.

— *Faint heart never won fair lady*: This means that you will not get the partner of your dreams if you lack the confidence to let them know how you feel.

— *Fair and square*: If someone wins something fair and square, they follow the rules and win conclusively.

— *Fair crack of the whip*: (UK) If everybody has a fair crack of the whip, they all have equal opportunities to do something.

— *Fair shake of the whip*: (USA) If everybody has a fair shake of the whip, they all have equal opportunities to do something.

- *Fair thee well*: Meaning completely and fully: I am tied up today to a fair-thee-well.
- *Fairweather friend*: A fairweather friend is the type who is always there when times are good but forgets about you when things get difficult or problems crop up.
- *Fall by the wayside*: To fall by the wayside is to give up or fail before completion.
- *Fall from grace*: If a person falls from grace, they lose favour with someone.
- *Game on*: When someone says 'Game on!', it means that they are accepting a challenge or ready to get something done.
- *Game plan*: A game plan is a strategy.
- *Garbage fee*: A garbage fee is a charge that has no value and doesn't provide any real service.
- *Garbage in, garbage out*: If a computer system or database is built badly, then the results will be bad.
- *Gardening leave*: (UK) If someone is paid for a period when they are not working, either after they have given in their notice or when they are being investigated, they are on gardening leave.
- *Gather pace*: If events gather pace, they move faster.
- *Gather steam*: If something gathers speed, it moves or progresses at an increasing speed.
- *Get a handle on*: When you get a handle on something, you come to understand it.
- *Get along famously*: If people get along famously, they have an exceedingly good relationship.

- *Get away scot-free*: If someone gets away scot-free, they are not punished when they have done something wrong.
- *Get away with murder*: If you get away with murder, you do something bad and don't get caught or punished.
- *Get back on the horse that bucked you*: When you start drinking again after being hungover from drinking the previous night.
- *Get in on the act*: If people want to get in on the act, they want to participate in something that is currently profitable or popular.
- *Get in on the ground floor*: If you get in on the ground floor, you enter a project or venture at the start before people know how successful it might be.
- *Get it in the neck*: (UK) If you get it in the neck, you are punished or criticised for something.
- *Get it off your chest*: If you get something off your chest, you confess to something that has been troubling you.
- *Get on your soapbox*: If someone on their soapbox, they hold forth (talk a lot) about a subject they feel strongly about.
- *Get out of bed on the wrong side*: If you get out of bed on the wrong side, you wake up and start the day in a bad mood for no real reason.
- *Hail-fellow-well-met*: Someone whose behaviour is hearty, friendly and congenial.
- *Hair of the dog*: If someone has a hair of the dog, they have an alcoholic drink as a way of getting

rid of a hangover, the unpleasant effects of having drunk too much alcohol the night before. It is commonly used as a way of excusing having a drink early on in the day.

- *Hairy at the heel*: (UK) Someone who is hairy at the heel is dangerous or untrustworthy.
- *Hale and hearty*: Someone who is hale and hearty is in very good health.
- *Half a mind*: If you have half a mind to do something, you haven't decided to do it, but are thinking seriously about doing it.
- *Half-baked*: A half-baked idea or scheme hasn't not been thought through or planned very well.
- *Hammer and tongs*: If people are going at it hammer and tongs, they are arguing fiercely. The idiom can also be used hen people are doing something energetically.
- *Hand in glove*: If people are hand in glove, they have an extremely close relationship.
- *Hand in hand*: Hand in hand= work together closely When people in a group, say in an office or in a project, work together with mutual understanding to achieve the target, we say they work hand in hand. There is no lack of co-operation and each synchoranises the activity with that of the other.
- *Hand that rocks the cradle*: Women have a great power and influence because they have the greatest influence over the development of children- the hand that rocks the cradle.

- *Hand to mouth*: Someone who's living from hand to mouth, is very poor and needs the little money they have coming in to cover their expenses.
- *Hands down*: If someone is better hands down than everyone else, they are much better.
- *Handwriting like chicken scratch*: If your handwriting is very hard to read, it is like chicken scratch.
- *Hang by a thread*: If something hangs by a thread, there is a very small chance indeed of it being successful or surviving.
- *Hang in the balance*: If an outcome is hanging in the balance, there are at least two possibilities and it is impossible to predict which will win out.
- *Hang out to dry*: If you hang someone out to dry, you abandon them when they are in trouble.
- *Hangdog expression*: A hangdog expression is one where the person's showing their emotions very clearly, maybe a little too clearly for your liking. It's that mixture of misery and self-pity that is similar to a dog when it's trying to get something it wants but daren't take without permission.
- *I hereby give notice of my intention*: Hereby is used sometimes in formal, official declarations and statements to give greater force to the speaker' or the writer's affirmation. People will say it sometimes to emphasise their sincerity and correctness.

- *I may be daft, but I'm not stupid*: I might do or say silly things occasionally, but in this instance I know what I am doing.
- *I should cocoa*: (UK) This idiom comes from 'I should think so', but is normally used sarcastically to mean the opposite.
- *I'll cross that road when I come to it*: I'll think about something just when it happens, not in advance.
- *I'll eat my hat*: You can say this when you are absolutely sure that you are right to let the other person know that there is no chance of your being wrong.
- *I've got a bone to pick with you*: If somebody says this, they mean that they have some complaint to make against the person they are addressing.
- *I've got your number*: You have made a mistake and I am going to call you on it. You are in trouble (a threat). I have a disagreement with you. I understand your true nature.
- *Icing on the cake*: This expression is used to refer to something good that happens on top of an already good thing or situation.
- *If the cap fits, wear it*: This idiom means that if the description is correct, then it is describing the truth, often when someone is being criticised.
- *If wishes were horses, beggars would ride*: This means that wishing for something or wanting it is not the same as getting or having it.
- *If wishes were horses, beggars would ride*: If we could have things the way we wanted them,

then life would be much easier than it is.

- *If you can't stand the heat, get out of the kitchen*: Originally a Harry S. Truman quote, this means that if you can't take the pressure, then you should remove yourself from the situation.
- *If you fly with the crows, you get shot with the crows*: If you wish to be associated with a particular high risk and/or high profile situation and benefit from the rewards of that association, you have to accept the consequences if things go wrong—you cannot dissociate yourself.
- *If you lie down with dogs, you will get up with fleas*: This means that if you become involved with bad company, there will be negative consequences.
- *If you lie down with the Devil, you will wake up in hell.*: This means that if you become involved with bad company, there will be negative consequences.
- *If you will*: 'If you will' is used as a way of making a concession in a sentence: He wasn't a very honest person, a liar if you will. Here, it is used a way of accepting that the reader or listener might think of the person as a liar, but without commit the writer or speaker to that position fully.
- *Jack Frost*: If everything has frozen in winter, then Jack Frost has visited.
- *Jack-of-all-trades*: A jack-of-all-trades is someone that can do many different jobs.
- *Jam on your face*: If you say that someone has jam on their face, they appear to be caught,

embarrassed or found guilty.

- *Jam tomorrow*: (UK) This idiom is used when people promise good things for the future that will never come.
- *Jane Doe*: Jane Doe is a name given to an unidentified female who may be party to legal proceedings, or to an unidentified person in hospital, or dead. John Doe is the male equivalent.
- *Kangaroo court*: When people take the law into their own hands and form courts that are not legal, these are known as kangaroo court.
- *Keen as mustard*: (UK) If someone is very enthusiastic, they are as keen as mustard.
- *Keep abreast*: If you keep abreast of things, you stay informed about developments.
- *Keep at bay*: If you keep someone or something at bay, you maintain a safe distance from them.
- *Keep body and soul together*: If you earn enough to cover your basic expenses, but nothing more than that, you earn enough to keep body and soul together.
- *Keep in touch*: If you keep in touch with someone, you keep communicating with them even though you may live far apart.
- *Keep it on the Q T*: If you keep something on the Q T, you keep it quiet or secret.
- *Keep it under your hat*: If you keep something under your hat, you keep it secret.
- *Labor of love*: A labor of love is a project or task

undertaking for the interest or pleasure in doing it rather than the reward, financial or otherwise.

- *Labour of love*: A labour of love is a project or task undertaking for the interest or pleasure in doing it rather than the reward, financial or otherwise.
- *Lame duck*: If something or someone is a lame duck, they are in trouble.
- *Land of nod*: If someone has gone to the land of nod, they have fallen asleep or gone to bed.
- *Landslide victory*: A landslide victory is a victory in an election by a very large margin.
- *Lap dog*: A lap dog is a person who is eager to please another at the expense of his or her own needs in order to maintain a position of privilege or favour.
- *Lap of the gods*: If something is in the lap of the gods, it is beyond our control and fate will decide the outcome.
- *Larger than life*: If something is excessive or exaggerated, it is larger than life.
- *Last hurrah*: If an elderly person does something special before they die, it is a last hurrah.
- *Last laugh*: The person who has the last laugh ends up with the the advantage in a situation after some setbacks.
- *Last straw*: The last straw is the final problem that makes someone lose their temper or the problem that finally brought about the collapse of something. It comes from an Arabic story,

where a camel was loaded with straw until a single straw placed on the rest of the load broke its back.

- *Last-ditch*: A last-ditch attempt is a desperate attempt that will probably fail anyway.
- *Laugh a minute*: Someone who is a laugh a minute is very funny.
- *Laugh to see a pudding crawl*: (UK) Someone who would laugh to see a pudding crawl is easily amused and will laugh at anything.
- *Laugh up your sleeve*: If you laugh up your sleeve, you laugh at someone secretly.
- *Laughing stock*: If someone becomes a laughing stock they do something so stupid or wrong that no one can take them seriously and people scorn and laugh at them.
- *Laughter is the best medicine*: Laughing is often helpful for healing, especially emotional healing.
- *Mad as a badger*: If someone is as mad as a badger, they are crazy.
- *Mad as a bag of hammers*: Someone who is as mad as a bag of hammers is crazy or stupid.
- *Mad as a cut snake*: (USA) One who is mad as a cut snake has lost all sense of reason, is crazy, out of control.
- *Mad as a hornet*: (USA) If someone is as mad as a hornet, they are very angry indeed.
- *Mad as a March hare*: Someone who is excitable and unpredictable is as mad as a March hare.
- *Made in the shade*: One has an easy time in life or

in a given situation. Finding things working to one's benefit.

- *Made of money*: If you are made of money, you have a lot of money.
- *Mailed fist*: Someone who rules or controls something with a mailed fist is in absolute control and tolerates no dissent. A mailed fist in a velvet glove is used to describe someone who appears soft on the outside, but underneath is very hard. 'Iron fist' is an alternative form.
- *Major league*: Something major league is very important.
- *Make a better fist*: If someone makes a better fist of doing something, they do a better job.
- *Make a clean breast*: If someone makes a clean breast, they confess in full to something they have done.
- *Make a killing*: If you make a killing, you do something that makes you a lot of money.
- *Make a meal*: If someone makes a meal of something, they spend too long doing it or make it look more difficult than it really is.
- *Make a mint*: If someone is making a mint, they are making a lot of money.
- *Make a monkey of someone*: If you make a monkey of someone, you make them look foolish.
- *Make a mountain out of a molehill*: If somebody makes a mountain out of a molehill, they exaggerate the importance or seriousness of a problem.

- *Make a pig's ear*: If you make a pig's ear of something, you make a mess of it.
- *Make a pitch*: If you make a pitch for something, you make a bid, offer or other attempt to get it.
- *Make a request*: If you request something, or make a request, you are asking for something you want or need.
- *Make a song and dance*: (UK) If someone makes a song and dance, they make an unecessary fuss about something unimportant.
- *Make an enquiry*: If you make an enquiry, you ask for general information about something.
- *Make bets in a burning house*: (USA) If people are making bets in a burning house, they are engaged in futile activity while serious problems around them are getting worse.
- *Make ends meet*: If somebody finds it hard to make ends meet, they have problems living on the money they earn.
- *Make hay*: If you make hay, or may hay while the sun shines, you take advantage of an opportunity as soon as it arises and do not waste time.
- *Make headway*: If you make headway, you make progress.
- *Make your toes curl*: If something makes your toes curl, it makes you feel very uncomfortable, shocked or embarrassed.
- *Man Friday*: From 'Robinson Crusoe', a 'Man Friday' refers to an assistant or companion,

usually a capable one. The common feminine equivalent is 'Girl Friday'.

- *Man of the cloth*: A man of the cloth is a priest.
- *Man proposes, God disposes*: Your fate lies in the hands of God.
- *Nail in the coffin*: A nail in someone or something's coffin is a problem or event that is a clear step towards an inevitable failure.
- *Nail-biter*: If a game, election, contest, etc, is a nail-biter, it is exciting because the competitors are so close that it is impossible to predict the result.
- *Nature abhors a vacuum*: This idiom is used to express the idea that empty or unfilled spaces are unnatural as they go against the laws of nature and physics.
- *Neck and neck*: If two competitors or candidates, etc, are neck and neck, then they are very close and neither is clearly winning.
- *Neck of the woods*: If someone talks about their neck of the woods, they mean the area where they live.
- *Need no introduction*: Someone who is very famous and known to everyone needs no introduction.
- *Needle in a haystack*: If trying to find something is like looking for a needle in a haystack, it means that it is very difficult, if not impossible to find among everything around it.
- *Neither fish nor fowl*: Something or someone that

is neither fish nor fowl doesn't really fit into any one group.

— *Neither here nor there*: If something is neither here nor there, it is of very little importance.

— *Neither use nor ornament*: Something that serves no purpose and is not aesthetically pleasing is neither use nor ornament.

— *Nerves of steel*: If someone has nerves of steel, they don't get frightened when other people do.

— *Object lesson*: An object lesson serves as a warning to others.

— *Odds and ends* L Odds and ends are small, remnant articles and things- the same as 'bits and bobs'.

— *Off colour*: If someone looks off colour/color, they look ill.

— *Off the scale*: If something goes off the scale, it far exceeds the normal standards, good or bad, for something.

— *Off the shelf*: If a product is off the shelf, it can be used straightaway without any setting-up.

— *Off the top of your head*: If you say something off the top of your head, you don't think about it beforehand.

— *Off the track*: If something puts or throws you off your track, it distracts you or keeps you from achieving what you want.

— *Off the wall*: Something that is off the wall is unconventional.

— *Off-hand*: Off-hand means without preparation.

People say that they don't know the answer off-hand, meaning that they don't know it at that time.

- *Oh, my goodness!*: An expression of surprise.
- *Old chestnut*: An old chestnut is something that has been repeated so many times that it has lost its impact.
- *Olive branch*: If you hold out or offer an olive branch, you make a gesture to indicate that you want peace.
- *On a fishing expedition*: If someone is on a fishing expedition, they are trying to get information, often using incorrect or improper ways to find things out.
- *On good terms*: If people are on good terms, they have a good relationship.
- *On the ball*: If someone's on the ball, they are well-informed and know what's going on in their area of responsibility or interest.
- *On the carpet*: When you are called to the bosses office (since supposedly, they are the only ones who have carpet) and its definitely not for a good reason, i.e., you are in trouble, something has not gone according to plan and either maybe you are responsible and/or have some explaining to do.
- *On the case*: If someone is on the case, they are dealing with a problem.
- *Pain in the neck*: If someone is very annoying and always disturbing you, they are a pain in the

neck. Pain in the butt, or pain in the ass (USA), and Pain in the arse (UK) are less polite alternative forms.

- *Pass the hat*: If you pass the hat, you ask a people in a group to give money.
- *Pen is mightier than the sword*: The idiom 'the pen is mightier than the sword' means that words and communication are more powerful than wars and fighting.
- *Penny pincher*: A penny pincher is a mean person or who is very frugal.
- *Perfidious Albion*: England is known to some as perfidious Albion, implying that it is not trustworthy in its dealings with foreigners.
- *Pick up the tab*: A person who pays for everyone picks up the tab.
- *Pick-up game*: (USA) A pick-up game is something unplanned where people respond to events as they happen.
- *Picture perfect*: When something is exactly as it should be it is said to be picture perfect.
- *Pie in the sky*: If an idea or scheme is pie in the sky, it is utterly impractical.
- *Piece of cake*: If something is a piece of cake, it is really easy.
- *Pieces of the same cake*: Pieces of the same cake are things that have the same characteristics or qualities.
- *Pig in a poke*: If someone buys a pig in a poke, they buy something without checking the

condition it was in, usually finding out later that it was defective.

- *Pigs might fly*: If you think something will never happen or succeed, you can say that 'pigs might fly' (or 'pigs can fly' and 'pigs will fly'- the idiom is used in many forms)
- *Pin down with a label*: If you pin someone down with a label, you characterise them, often meant negatively as the label is restrictive.
- *Plain as the nose on your face*: If something is as plain as the nose on your face, it is very clear and obvious.
- *Plain Jane*: A plain Jane is a woman who isn't particularly attractive.
- *Plain sailing*: If something is relatively easy and there are no problems doing it, it is plain sailing.
- *Play for keeps*: If you are playing for keeps, you take things very seriously and the outcome is very important to you; it is not a mere game.
- *Play hardball*: If someone plays hardball, they are very aggressive in trying to achieve their aim.
- *Play the field*: Someone who plays the field has sexual relationships with many people.
- *Queen bee*: The queen bee is a woman who holds the most important position in a place.
- *Queen of Hearts*: A woman who is pre-eminent in her area is a Queen of Hearts.
- *Queer Street*: If someone is in a lot of trouble, especially financial, they are in Queer Street.
- *Queer your pitch*: If someone queers your pitch,

they interfere in your affairs and spoil things.

- *Question of time*: If something's a question of time, it's certain to happen, though we don't know exactly when.
- *Queue jumping*: Someone who goes to the front of a queue instead of waiting is jumping the queue.
- *Quick as a flash*: If something happens quick as a flash, it happens very fast indeed.
- *Quiet as a cat*: If somebody is as quiet as a cat they make as little noise as possible and try to be unnoticeable.
- R
- *Rack and ruin*: If something or someone goes to rack and ruin, they are utterly destroyed or wrecked.
- *Rack your brain*
- If you rack your brain, you think very hard when trying to remember something.
- *Rack your brain*: If you rack your brain, you think hard, especially when trying to remember something or find a solution.
- *Rags to riches*: Someone who starts life very poor and becomes rich goes from rags to riches.
- *Rain on your parade*: If someone rains on your parade, they ruin your pleasure or your plans.
- *Raining cats and dogs*: When it is raining cats and dogs, it is raining very heavily.
- *Rainy day*: If you save something, especially

money, for a rainy day, you save it for some possible problem or trouble in the future.

- *Raise eyebrows*: If something raises eyebrows, it shocks or surprises people.
- *Real deal*: If something is the real deal, it is genuine and good.
- *Real McCoy*: Something that's the real McCoy is the genuine article, not a fake.
- *Real plum*: A real plum is a good opportunity.
- *Real trooper*: A real trooper is someone who will fight for what they believe in and doesn't give up easily.
- *Recharge your batteries*: If you recharge your batteries, you do something to regain your energy after working hard for a long time.
- *Recipe for disaster*: A recipe for disaster is a mixture of people and events that could only possibly result in trouble.
- *Red carpet*: If you give someone the red-carpet treatment, you give them a special welcome to show that you think they are important. You can roll out the red carpet, too.
- *Red herring*: If something is a distraction from the real issues, it is a red herring.
- *Sacred cow*: Something that is a sacred cow is held in such respect that it cannot be criticised or attacked.
- *Safe and sound*: If you arrive safe and sound, then nothing has harmed you on your way.
- *Safe bet*: A proposition that is a safe bet doesn't

have any risks attached.

- *Safe pair of hands*: A person who can be trusted to do something without causing any trouble is a safe pair of hands.
- *Safety in numbers*: If a lot of people do something risky at the same time, the risk is reduced because there is safety in numbers.
- *Salty dog*: A salty dog is an experienced sailor.
- *Same old, same old*: When nothing changes, it's the same old, same old.
- *Save face*: If someone saves face, they manage to protect their reputation.
- *Save someone's bacon*: If something saves your bacon, it saves your life or rescues you from a desperate situation. People can also save your bacon.
- *Say when*: People say this when pouring a drink as a way of telling you to tell them when there's enough in your glass.
- *Scare the daylights out of someone*: If you scare the daylights out of someone, you terrify them.
- *Scarlet woman*: This idiom is used as a pejorative term for a sexually promiscuous woman, especially an adulteress.
- *Scotch Mist*: The phrase 'Scotch mist' is used humorously to refer to something that is hard to find or doesn't exist—something imagined.
- *Seamy side*: The seamy side of something is the unpleasant or sordid aspect it has.
- *See red*: If someone sees red, they become very

angry about something.

- *See the elephant*: If you see the elephant, you experience much more than you wish to; it is often used when a soldier goes into a warzone for the first time.
- *See you later*: A casual way of saying to friends I'll see you again, sometime,—this is often abbreviated to 'Later' or 'Laters' as an alternative way of saying goodbye.
- *Seeing is believing*: This idiom means that people can only really believe what they experience personally.
- *Seen better days*: If something's seen better days, it has aged badly and visibly compared to when it was new. The phrase can also be used to describe people.
- *Tables are turned*: When the tables are turned, the situation has changed giving the advantage to the party who had previously been at a disadvantage.
- *Tackle an issue*: If you tackle an issue or problem, you resolve or deal with it.
- *Take a hike*: This is a way of telling someone to get out.
- *Take a raincheck*: If you take a rain check, you decline an offer now, suggesting you will accept it later.
- *Take guts*: If something takes guts, it requires courage in the face of danger or great risk. It takes guts for firemen to enter a burning

building to save someone.

— *Take someone to task*: If you take someone to task, you scold them for something they have done wrong.

— *Take the chair*: If you take the chair, your become the chairman or chairwoman of a committee, etc.

— *Take the fall*: If you tall the fall, you accept the blame and possibly the punishment for another's wıongdoing, with the implication that the true culprit, for political or other reasons, cannot be exposed as guilty.

— *Take the plunge*: If you take the plunge, you decide to do something or commit yourself even though you know there is an element of risk involved.

— *Take the rough with the smooth*: People say that you have to take the rough with the smooth, meaning that you have to be prepared to accept the disadvantages as well of the advantages of something.

— *Take to your heels*: If you take to your heels, you run away.

— *Take up the torch*: If you take up the torch, you take on a challenge or responsibility, usually when someone else retires, or leaves an organisation, etc.

— *Take your breath away*: If something takes your breath away, it astonishes or surprises you.

— *Take your eye off the ball*: If someone takes their eye off the ball, they don't concentrate on something important that they should be looking at.

- *Take your hat off*: If you say that you take your hat off to someone, you are showing your respect or admiration.
- *Take your hat off to somebody*: If you take your hat off to someone, you acknowledge that they have done something exceptional or otherwise deserve your respect.
- *Talk of the town*: When everybody is talking about particular people and events, they are he talk of the town.
- *Talk turkey*: When people talk turkey, they discuss something frankly.
- *Tar baby*: A tar baby is a problem that gets worse when people try to sort it out.
- *Teeny-weeny*: If something is teensy-weensy, it is very small indeed.
- *U-turn*: If a government changes its position radically on an issue, especially when they have promised not to do so, this is a U-turn.
- *Uncharted waters*: If you're in uncharted waters, you are in a situation that is unfamiliar to you, that you have no experience of and don't know what might happen.
- *Under a cloud*: If someone is suspected of having done something wrong, they are under a cloud.
- *Under a flag of convenience*: If a ship sails under a flag of convenience, it is registered in a country where taxes, etc, are lower than in the country it

comes from, so if someone does something under a flag of convenience, they attempt to avoid regulations and taxes by a similar means.

- *Under false colours*: If someone does something under false colours/colors, they pretend to be something they are not in order to deceive people so that they can succeed.
- *Under fire*: If someone is being attacked and cricitised heavily, they are under fire.
- *Under lock and key*: If something is under lock and key, it is stored very securely.
- *Under someone's heel*: If you are under someone's heel, they have complete control over you.
- *Under the radar*: If something slips under the radar, it isn't detected or noticed.
- *Under the table*: Bribes or illegal payments are often described as money under the table.
- *Under the weather*: If you are feeling a bit ill, sad or lack energy, you are under the weather.
- *Under your belt*: If you have something under your belt, you have already achieved or experienced it and it will probably be of benefit to you in the future.
- *Under your breath*: If you say something under your breath, you whisper or say it very quietly.
- *Under your nose*: If something happens right in front of you, especially if it is surprising or audacious, it happens under your nose.
- *Under your skin*: If someone gets under your skin, they really annoy you.

— *Vale of tears*: This vale of tears is the world and the suffering that life brings.

— *Velvet glove*: This idiom is used to describe a person who appears gentle, but is determined and inflexible underneath.

— *Vent your spleen*: If someone vents their spleen, they release all their anger about something.

— *Vicious circle*: A vicious circle is a sequence of events that make each other worse- someone drinks because they are unhappy at work, then loses their job... 'Vicious cycle' is also used.

— *Virgin territory*: If something is virgin territory, it hasn't been explored before.

— *Volte-face*: If you do a volte-face on something, you make a sudden and complete change in your stance or position over an issue.

— *Wag the dog*: To 'wag the dog' means to purposely divert attention from what would otherwise be of greater importance, to something else of lesser significance. By doing so, the lesser-significant event is catapulted into the limelight, drowning proper attention to what was originally the more important issue. The expression comes from the saying that 'a dog is smarter than its tail', but if the tail were smarter, then the tail would 'wag the dog'. The expression 'wag the dog' was elaborately used as theme of the movie. 'Wag the Dog', a 1997 film starring Robert de Niro and Dustin Hoffman, produced and directed by Barry Levinson.

— *Wait for a raindrop in the drought*: When someone is waiting for a raindrop in the drought, they are waiting or hoping for something that is extremely unlikely to happen.

— *Waiting in the wings*: If someone is waiting in the wings, or in the wings, they are in the background, but nearby, ready to act on short notice.

— *Wake up and smell the coffee*: When someone doesn't realise what is really happening or is not paying enough attention to events around them, you can tell them to wake up and smell the coffee.

— *Wake-up call*: A wake-up call is a warning of a threat or a challenge, especially when it means that people will have to change their behaviour to meet it.

— *Walk a fine line*: If you have to walk a fine line, you have to be very careful not to annoy or anger people or groups that are competing.

— *Yah boo sucks*: Yah boo & yah boo sucks can be used to show that you have no sympathy with someone.

— *Yank my chain*: If some one says this to another person (i.e. stop yanking my chain) it means for the other person to leave the person who said it alone and to stop bothering them.

— *Young blood*: Young people with new ideas and fresh approaches are young blood.

— *Young Turk*: A Young Turk is a young person who is rebellious and difficult to control in a company, team or organisation.

— *Your belly button is bigger than your stomach*: If

your belly button is bigger than your stomach, you take on more responsibilities than you can handle.

- *Your call*: If something is your call, it is up to you to make a decision on the matter.
- *Your name is mud*: If someone's name is mud, then they have a bad reputation.
- *Your sins will find you out*: This idiom means that things you do wrong will become known.
- *Zero hour*: The time when something important is to begin is zero hour.
- *Zero tolerance*: If the police have a zero tolerance policy, they will not overlook any crime, no matter how small or trivial.
- *Zigged before you zagged*: If you did things in the wrong order, you zigged before you zagged.

5

Word Order

The Word Order is a must for every sentence. The words in a sentence should be put in a proper order so that the intended meaning is understood. Sometimes, the order in which a set of words is used in a sentence can give rise to ambiguity. And they should be reordered to bring out the intended meaning clearly.

Example-1:

— A nursemaid is wanted to look after a baby about twenty-years old.

In this sentence it is not clear who is twenty-year old?

Whether the nursemaid or the baby?

Certainly it is only the nursemaid. So the proper word-order is:

— A nursemaid, about twenty-years old, is wanted to look after a baby.

Example-2:

— After the accident, I was for thirty days confined to the cot with swollen legs.

Here also it is not clear, who had the swollen legs?

Whether I or the cot?

Certainly it is only I.

So the correct sentence is:

— After the accident, I was confined with swollen legs to the cot for thirty days.

Example-3:

— The stool over there was purchased by my grandfather with three legs.

Here also who has three legs?

Whether the stool or my grandfather?

Certainly it is only the stool.

So the correct sentence is:

— The stool, with three legs, over there was purchased by my grandfather.

Example-4:

— These verses were written by a young man who has long since been dead for his own amusement.

The correct sentence is:

— These verses were written by a young man for his amusement, but he was long since been dead.

Example-5:

— You must not forget to visit the spot where Gandhi was assassinated during your trip to Delhi.

The correct word order is:

— During your trip to Delhi, You must not forget to visit the spot where Gandhi was assassinated.

Example-6:

— The man was brought before the Judge who had stolen the watch.

The correct word order is:

— The man, who had stolen the watch, was brought before the Judge.

Example-7:

— A publication may be used in any state where it regularly circulates under a unanimous ruling by the Supreme Court.

The correct word order is:

— Under a unanimous ruling by the Supreme Court, a publication may be sued for libel in any state in which it circulates.

Example-8:

— Promotions, retirements, deaths and other actions approved by the board of directors at its May meeting will be reported in the July issue of the company paper.

The correct word order is:

— The July issue of the company paper will report on Promotions, retirements and other actions approved by the board of directors at its May meeting; the paper will also include obituaries.

These examples might have made the point very clear that the proper word-order is must for any sentence to be beautiful.

USE OF WORDS

In this section, miscellaneous types of Use of Words are discussed in detail.

Use of At least when referring to a number:

The phrase at least 50 percent is preferable to the phrase 50 per cent or more than 50 per cent. Similarly, the phrases 'maximum of 50 percent' and 'at the most 50 per cent' are preferred to the phrase '50 per cent or less than 50 per cent'.

Example-1:

— Several studies have found that the corollary patients who exercise most actively have half or less than half the chance of dying of a heart attack as those who are sedentary.

This sentence is wrong one.

The correct sentence is:

— Several studies have found that the corollary patients who exercise most actively are at least fifty percent less likely than those who are sedentary to die of a heart attack.

Use of the article THE in relation to a specific number.

Normally, we do not add the definite article THE to a number.

Examples:

— There are 78 students in our class.

— I secured 90marks out of 100 in the English test.

But, the use of the article is required when a section of a known number of persons or things is referred to.

Example-1:

— In the last test, 70 out of the 100 students in my class received more than 90%.

— Only 6 out of the 37 colleges in this city are coeducational.

Became twice or doubled:

The single word doubled is preferable to the two-word term became twice:

Examples:

— The number of undergraduate degrees in the engineering awarded by colleges and Universities in USA increased more than twice from 1990 to 1998.

The correct sentence is:

— The number of undergraduate degrees in the engineering awarded by colleges and Universities in USA more than doubled from 1990 to 1998.

Between should always be complemented by and:

When an event happens between two specific times, say 2 o'clock and 4o'clock, we should use either the phrase between 2 o'clock and 4o'clock or the phrase from 2o'clock to 4o'clock.

Similarly the phrases BETWEEN....WITH, BETWEEN...AS and BETWEEN...AT are wrong ones.

This rules allies not only to sentences relating to time but whenever BETWEEBN is used.

Examples:

— My house lies halfway between the park and the post office.

— Between Ram and Clinton, the former is older.

Word DISTINGUISH must always be complemented by FROM:

Examples:

— Clinton is an avid stamp collector, and is an expert in distinguishing genuine stamps from fake ones.

— Gemologists are taught to distinguish real pearls from cultured ones.

Use of IF and WHETHER.

The word IF should be used only as a conditional conjunction and not as a conjunction indicating a choice.

Examples:

— I shall go the movie only if you also come with me.

— If it does not rain, we shall go on a picnic next Sunday.

Where a choice of action is indicated, the proper word to be used is WHETHER, not IF.

Examples:

— We have been debating whether we should go to New York or to Chicago.

— The election commission has not yet decided on whether to hold the poll in June or in July.

Use of the phrase W,X,Y and Z:

When three or nouns or verbs are used in a sentence in serial, those except the last one must be separated by a comma, and the conjunction 'and' must be added before the last.

Example:

- I was accompanied to College by Clinton, George, Mary and Charles.

The following versions are wrong ones:

- I was accompanied to College by Clinton, George, Mary, Charles.
- I was accompanied to College by Clinton and George, Mary, Charles.
- I was accompanied to College by Clinton and George, Mary and Charles.

QUANTITY WORDS

Words which are denoting the quantity of the nouns are called Quantity-Words.

English has different adjectives to describe countable words and uncountable words.

Examples of countable nouns are:

- Boys, men, elephants, questions, tables, shirts, computers etc...

Examples of Uncountable nouns:

- Water, fire, rain, dress, sugar, sky, thirsty etc...

Different set of words should be used as adjectives in respect of countable nouns and uncountable nouns.

- *Countable nouns*: Fewer, number of, many etc...
- *Uncountable nouns*: Less, amount, quantity, much, more etc...

Using the adjective 'fewer', 'number of' and 'many' for noun-countable nouns is wrong.

Similarly, using the adjectives ' less', 'amount', 'quantity' and 'much' in respect of countable nouns is also wrong.

Example-1:

— Less boys than girls passed the test.

Here the adjective 'less' has been used for the countable noun 'boys'. This usage is wrong one.

The correct sentence is:

— Fewer boys than girls passed the test.

Example-2:

— I like fewer sugar in coffee than in tea.

Here, the adjective 'fewer' has been used for the uncountable noun 'sugar'. This usage is wrong one.

The correct sentence is:

— I like less sugar in coffee than in tea.

Example-3:

— The number of delegates who attended the conference exceeded the estimate.

Here also, the wrong adjective has been used for the countable noun 'delegates' in place of the adjective 'number'

The correct sentence is:

— The amount of delegates who attended the conference exceeded the estimate.

These are perfect examples for the usages of Quantity-Words.

Example-4:

— The book sold 10,000 copies in hard cover, and almost thrice as much in paper-pack.

Here also the adjective 'much' has been used for the countable noun 'books' in place of the adjective 'many'.

So the correct sentence is:

— The book sold 10,000 copies in hard cover, and almost thrice as many in paper-pack.

Example-5:

— The army had twenty less divisions two years ago that It has now.

Here also, the adjective 'less' has been used for the countable noun 'divisions' in place of the adjective 'fewer'.

The correct sentence is:

— The army had twenty fewer divisions two years ago that It has now.

These are perfect examples for the usages of Quantity-Words.

Examples:

— Much of the words spoken by the speaker could not be heard because of the din.

— Many of the words spoken by the speaker could not be heard because of the din.

— I have less pants than shirts.

— I have fewer pants than shirts.

Use of 'between' and 'among':

— The preposition 'between' and 'among' can not be substituted for each other.

— The preposition 'between' should be used only when there are two items referred to.

— When there are more than two items, the correct preposition to be used is 'among'.

Examples:

— Among Clinton and George, it is George who is older. (Incorrect)

— Between Clinton and George, it is George who is older. (Correct)

— Between the three girls, Anne is the tallest. (Incorrect)

— Among the three girls, Anne is the tallest. (Correct)

— Between Asia, Africa and America, Asia has the largest area. (Incorrect)

— Among Asia, Africa and America, Asia has the largest area. (Correct)

— Among, the Indian and Korean, the former is usually taller than the latter. (Incorrect)

— Between, the Indian and Korean, the former is usually taller than the latter. (Correct)

These are perfect examples for the usages of Quantity-Words.

Use of 'each other' and 'one another':

Similarly 'each other' must be used while referring to only two persons.

When there are more than two persons, the correct phrase to be used is 'one another'.

Examples:

— The two brothers are so different that they have nothing in common with one another. (Incorrect)

- The two brothers are so different that they have nothing in common with each other. (Correct)
- Ten of us study together for the test, and we help each other with the lessons. (Incorrect)
- Ten of us study together for the test, and we help one another with the lessons. (Correct)

These are perfect examples for the usages of Quantity-Words.

Comparative and Superlative degrees:

English are different forms of comparisons when two nouns are compared and when more than two nouns are compared.

Example-1:

- Between Clinton and George, the former is the tallest.

Here only two nouns are compared so only the Comparative Degree of Comparison should be used in place of Superlative Degree of Comparison.

The correct sentence is:

- Between Clinton and George, the former is taller.

While using the superlative degree of comparison, you should always use 'the' before it. These are perfect examples for the usages of Quantity-Words.

Examples:

- Copal is tallest student in the class. (Incorrect)
- Copal is the tallest student in the class. (Correct)
- She is most loyal among all the staff in the company. (Incorrect)

— She is the most loyal among all the staff in the company (Correct)

These examples might have revealed the secrets of using the right Quantity-words in your sentences.

FORMATION OF WORDS

The Formation of Words has few rules which determine the nature of the words formed thus. Words can be classified into four types as follows:

1. Primary Words.
2. Compound Words
3. Primary Derivatives
4. Secondary Derivatives

Now, let us see how each type of word is formed.

Primary Words:

Words which are not derived or compounded or developed from other words are called Primary Words. They belong to the original stocks of the words.

Examples:

— Most of the words in English language are only Primary Words.

— Moon, sun, day, night, month, school, boy, girl, road, write, go sit, walk, net, dash, dot, book, pin, he, she, it etc...

— A Primary Word may be of the type of noun, verb, adjective, pronoun, adverb etc...

— The Formation of Words has few rules which determine the nature of the words formed thus.

Compound Words:

The Compound Words are formed by joining two or more Primary Words.

Examples:

— Moonlight, undertake, nevertheless, man-of-war, misunderstanding etc...

— This way the Compound Words are formed.

— A Compound Word may be of the type of noun, verb, adjective, pronoun, adverb, conjunction, preposition etc...

— An addition to the beginning of a word is a Prefix.

— An addition to the end of word is a Suffix.

— Compound Words are the most part Nouns, Adjectives and Verbs

Now let us we how the Compound Words of Nouns, Adjectives and Verbs are formed.

Compound Words-Nouns:

Compound Words-Nouns may be formed:

i. Noun + Noun:

Examples:

— Moonlight

— Armchair

— Postman

— Railway

— Shoemaker

— Windmill

- Teaspoon
- Haystack
- Ringleader
- Jailbird
- Horse-power
- Screwdriver
- Tax-payer
- Airman
- Manservant
- Fire-escape
- Chess-board

ii. Adjective + Noun:

Examples:

- Sweetheart
- Nobleman
- Shorthand
- Blackboard
- Quicksilver
- Stronghold
- Halfpenny

iii. Verb + Noun:

Examples:

- Spendthrift
- Makeshift
- Breakfast
- Telltale

— Pick-packet
— Cut-throat
— Daredevil
— Hangman
— Scarecrow

The Formation of Words has few rules which determine the nature of the words formed thus.

iv. Gerund + Noun:

Examples:

— Drawing-room
— Writing-desk
— Looking-glass
— Walking-stick
— Blotting-paper
— Stepping-stone
— Spelling-book

v. Adverb (or Preposition)+ Noun:

Examples:

— Outlaw
— Afternoon
— Forethought
— Foresight
— Overcoat
— Downfall
— Afternoon
— Bypass

- Inmate
- Inside

vi. Verb + Adverb:

Examples:

- Drawback
- Lock-up
- Go-between
- Die-hard
- Send-off

vii. Adverb + Verb:

Knowledge of Formation of words will help you form your own words.

Examples:

- Outset
- Upkeep
- Outcry
- Income
- Outcome

Compound Words-Adjectives:

i. Noun + Adjectives (or Participle):

Examples:

- Blood-red
- Sky-blue
- Snow-white
- Pitch-dark

— Breast-high
— Skin-deep
— Lifelong
— World-wide
— Headstrong
— Homesick
— Stone-blind
— Seasick
— Love-lorn
— Hand-made
— Bed-ridden
— Heart-broken
— Moth-eaten
— Note-worthy

Knowledge of Formation of words will help you form your own words.

ii. Adjective + Adjective:

Examples:

— Red-hot
— Blue-black
— White-hot
— Dull-grey
— Lukewarm

iii. Adverb + Participle:

Examples:

— Longsuffering

— Everlasting
— Never-ending
— Thorough-bred
— Well-deserved
— Outspoken
— Down-hearted
— Inborn
— Far-seen

iv. Noun + Verb:

— Waylay
— Backbite
— Typewrite
— Browbeat
— Earmark

v. Adjective + Verb:

Examples:

— Safeguard
— Whitewash
— Fulfill

vi. Adverb + Verb:

Examples:

— Overthrow
— Overtake
— Foretell
— Undertake
— Undergo

— Overhear
— Overdo
— Outbid
— Outdo
— Upset
— Ill-use

The Formation of Words has few rules which determine the nature of the words formed thus.

In most Compound Words, it is the first word which modifies the meaning of the second word. The accent is placed upon the modifying word when the amalgamation is complete. When the two elements are only partially blended, a hyphen is put between the two words and the accent fall equally on both of them.

Primary Derivatives:

These words are formed by making some changes in the body of the Primary Words.

— Bond from bind
— Breach from break
— Wrong from wring

The most important class of words formed by internal changes consists of the past tenses of the Primary Words. Those past tense-words are not treated as Derivatives.

i. Formation of Nouns from Verbs:

Examples:

— Choice from choose

- Bliss from bless
- Chip from chop
- Breach from break
- Dole from deal
- Dike from dig
- Fleet from float
- Doom from deem
- Bier from bear
- Watch from wake
- Seat from sit
- Gap from gape
- Girth from gird
- Grief from grieve
- Woof from weave

ii. Formation of Nouns from Adjectives:

Examples:

- Dolt from dull
- Heat from hot
- Pride from proud

iii. Formation of Adjectives from Verbs:

Examples:

- Fleet from float
- Low from lie

iv. Formation of Adjectives from Nouns:

Examples:

- Milch from milk

— Wise from wit

v. Formation of Verbs from Nouns:

Examples:

— Bathe from bath
— Bleed from blood
— Believe from belief
— Breathe from breath
— Breed from brood
— Clothe from cloth
— Drip from drop
— Feed from food

The Formation of Words has few rules which determine the nature of the words formed thus.

vi. Formation of Adjectives from Verbs:

Examples:

— Cool from chill
— Hale from heal

vii. Formation of Nouns from Verbs:

Examples:

— Gold from gild
— Grass from graze
— Half from halve
— Knot from knit
— Sale from sell
— Sooth from soothe
— Tale from tell

— Thief from thieve
— Wreath from wreathe

Secondary Derivatives:

Secondary derivatives of a word are formed by adding either a prefix or a suffix to the word.

An addition to the beginning of a word is a Prefix.

An addition to the end of word is a Suffix.

Examples:

— Income is a secondary derivative of the word 'word'.
— Here the addition 'in' is a prefix.
— Undergo is a secondary derivative of the word 'go'.
— Here the addition 'under' is a prefix.
— Friendship is a secondary derivative of the word friend.
— Here the addition 'ship' is a suffix.
— Darkness is a secondary derivative of the word 'dark'.
— Here the addition 'ness' is a suffix.

There are many prefixes and suffixes. The Formation of Words has few rules which determine the nature of the words formed thus.

6

Figures of Speech

The Figure of Speech is departure from the ordinary form of expression, or the ordinary course of ideas in order to produce a greater effect.

Figure-of-Speech may be classified as under:

1. Those based on resemblance:
   - Simile
   - Metaphor
   - Personification
   - Apostrophe
2. Those based on Contrast:
   - Antithesis
   - Epigram
3. Those based on Association:
   - Metonymy
   - Synecdoche
4. Thos depending on Construction:
   - Climax
   - Anticlimax

Let us see one by one.

SIMILE

Similes are a specific and formulaic form of allegory. A simile is a juxtaposed comparison of two or more objects to draw attention to their similarities. In English, similes are typically marked by use of like or as or than or resembles. Similes show how two things, that are not alike in most ways, are similar in one important way. Similes are a way to describe something. Authors use them to make their writing more interesting or entertaining.

A popular mnemonic for a simile is that a simile is similar or alike.

Examples:

1. Playing chess with Ashley is like trying to outsmart a computer.

The activity playing chess with Ashley is being compared to trying to outsmart a computer. The point is that Ashley can think in a powerful manner that resembles the way a computer operates, not that she is like a computer in any other way.

2. His temper was as explosive as a volcano.

His temper is being compared to a volcano in that it can be sudden and violent.

Few more examples of similes:

— Walking onto those sun-warmed stones was like stepping onto a hot plate.

— The cat, quick as lightning, pounced on the rat.

— She's as dull as a doorknob.

Similes have been widely used in literature for their expressiveness as a figure of speech:

- Curley was flopping like a fish on a line.
- The very mist on the Essex marshes was like a gauzy and radiant fabric.
- Why, man, he doth bestride the narrow world like a Colossus.

In Simile, a comparison is made between two object of different kinds which have at least one point in common.

The Simile is introduced by the word 'as...as'.

Examples:

- As active as quicksilver
- As afraid as a grasshopper
- As ageless as the sun
- As agile as a cat
- As agile as a monkey
- As alert as a bird
- As alike as two peas
- As alone as a leper
- As alone as Crusoe
- As ambitious as the devil

This Figure-of-Speech is widely used by us in our writings.

Note: A comparison of two things of same kind is not a Simile.

METAPHOR

A Metaphor is an implied Simile. It does not, like a Simile, state that one thing is like another or acts as another, but takes that for granted and proceeds as if two things were one.

Thus when we say, 'He fought as fiercely as a lion', it is Simile.

But when we say, 'He was a lion in the fight', it is Metaphor.

Examples:

- The camel is the ship of the desert.
- Life is a dream.
- The news was a dragger to his heart.
- Revenge is a kind of wild justice.

Note: Every SIMILE can be compressed into a METAPHOR, and Every METAPHOR can be expanded into a SIMILE.

Examples:

- Richard fought as fiercely as a loin. (Simile)
- Richard was a lion in the fight. (Metaphor)
- The waves thundered on the shore. (Metaphor)
- The waves broke on the shore with noise like a thunder.

This Figure-of-Speech is also widely used by us in our writings.

PERSONIFICATION

In Personification, inanimate objects and abstract notions are spoken of as having life and intelligence.

Examples:

- Death lays its icy hands on King.
- Pride goes forth on horseback, grand and gay.

— Laughter is holding her both sides.

APOSTROPHE

An Apostrophe is a direct address to the dead, to the absent, or to a personified object or idea. This figure is a special form of Personification.

Examples:

— Milton! You should not be living at this hour.

— Friend! I know not which way I must look for comfort.

— Roll on! Thou deep and dark blue Ocean, roll.

— Death! Where is thy sting? O Grave! Where is thy victory?

This Figure-of-Speech is also widely used by us in our writings.

HYPERBOLE

In Hyperbole, a statement is made emphatic by overstatement.

Examples:

— Why, man, if the river is dry, I am able to fill it with tears.

— Hmalet! You have not cleft my heart in twain.

EUPHEMISM

Euphemism consists in the description of a disagreeable thing by an agreeable name.

Examples:

— You are telling me a fairy tale. (You are telling me lies)

— He is gone to heaven. (He is dead)

This Figure-of-Speech is also widely used by us in our writings.

ANTITHESIS

In Antithesis, a striking opposition or contrast of words or sentiments is made in the same sentence. It is employed to secure emphasis.

Examples:

— Man proposes, but God disposes.

— Not that I loved Caesar less, but I loved Rome more.

— Speech is silver, but Silence is Gold.

— Many are called, but few are chosen.

— To err is human, but to forgive on divine.

OXYMORON

Oxymoron is special type of Antithesis, whereby two contradictory qualities are predicted at once of the same thing.

Examples:

— She accepted it as the kind cruelty of surgeon's knife.

— His honor rooted in dishonor stood.

— Faith unfaithful kept him falsely true.

— So innocent arch, so cunningly simple.

Here is the largest collection of the Top Favorite Oxymorons.

— Accurate Estimate
— Act Naturally
— Adult Child
— Agree to Disagree
— All Alone
— Anti-Missile Missile
— Appear Invisible
— Assistant Supervisor
— Awfully Nice
— Better than New
— Big Baby
— Bigger Half
— Birth Control
— Black Comedy
— Born Again (Christian)
— Born Dead
— Boxing Ring
— Bride groom
— Brief Speech
— Brief Survey
— Buffalo Wings
— Business Ethics
— Business Party
— Butt head
— Calm Storm
— Casual Chic

- Cat fish
- Chili (Refers to hot)
- Civil War
- Climb Down
- Commercial Art
- Completed Research
- Confirmed Rumor
- Consistently Inconsistent
- Constant Change
- Constant Variable
- Copyrighted Fake
- Corporate Family
- Cruel Kindness
- Current History
- Daily Special
- Day Dreams
- Dead Livestock
- Deliberate Mistake
- Deregulation Law
- Dick Head
- Dim wit
- Distant Relative
- Doing Nothing
- Drawing a Blank
- Dress Shirt
- Drive-Thru Window

- Dry Beer
- Dry Ice
- Easy Labor (Childbirth)
- Educational Television
- Expect the Unexpected
- Expressive Silence
- Extra ordinary
- Eyes Wide Shut
- False Evidence
- False Fact
- Farewell Reception
- Fatal Attraction
- Fat-Free Ice Cream
- Fiber Glass
- Fighting for Peace
- Final Draft
- First Conclusions
- Flexible Budget
- Fresh Dried Fruit
- Friendly Fire (From own military side)
- Full Vacuum (Bag)
- Global Village
- Going Nowhere
- Gold Silverware
- Graduate Student
- Grand Children

- Growing Small
- Hate to Hate
- Here and There
- Historical Event
- Holy Crap
- Holy War
- Home Office
- Home work
- Hot Chili
- Humane War
- Include Me Out
- Invisible Ink
- Jumbo Shrimp
- Junk Food
- Just Friends
- Known Secret
- Least Favorite
- Liquid Gas
- Little Big
- Live Recording
- Live Television
- Local Network
- Long Shorts
- Love Crime
- Low Fat
- Major General

- Martial Arts
- Medium Well
- Mercy Killing
- Misanthropic Philanthropist
- Mobile House
- Mobile Station
- Modern History
- Mud Bath
- Natural Additives
- Natural Makeup
- Never Generalise
- New Classic
- New Used Cars
- New and Improved
- No Comment (Is a Comment)
- No Means Yes
- Now and Then
- Objective Opinion
- Old Boy
- Old News
- One Man Show
- Peace Force
- Peacekeeping Force
- Pepper Cherry
- Perfect Mismatch
- Personal Business

- Plastic Glasses
- Practical Joke
- Preliminary Conclusion
- Pretty Bad
- Public Opinion
- Random Pattern
- Re- creation
- Real Fake
- Real Polyester
- Real Potential
- Real TV
- Reality TV
- Real-Life Show
- Relaxation Exercise
- Rush Hour (Heavy traffic period)
- Sad Smile
- Saying Nothing
- Science Fiction
- Selfish Lover
- Sharp Curve
- Show Business
- Single Parent
- Singles Club
- Small Crowd
- Small Fortune
- Smart Ass

— Sopho more (Wise fool)
— Specialise in Everything
-- Steel Wool
— Sugarless Candy
— Suicide Victim
— Sweet and Sour
— Talk Show
— Tears of Joy
— Terribly Good
— Thinking out Loud
— Timeless Moment
— Top Floor
— Tough Love
— Train the Trainer
— True Story (Stories)
— United Nations
— Vegetarian Hamburger
— Very Little
— Virtual Reality
— Wall Street
— War Games
— Well-Known Secret
— We're Alone
— White Chocolate
— White Gold
— Whole some

— Wireless Cable
— Working Mother

EPIGRAM

An Epigram is a brief pointed saying frequently introducing antithetical ideas which excite surprise and arrest attention.

Examples:

— The child is the father of the man.
— Fools rush in where angels fear to tread.
— In the midst of life, we are in death.
— Art lies in concealing art.
— He makes no friend who never made a foe.
— A man can not be too careful in the choice of his enemies.
— The proper study of mankind is man.

IRONY

Irony is made of speech in which the real meaning is exactly the opposite of that which is literally conveyed.

Examples:

— No doubts but you are the people, and wisdom shall die with you.

This Figure-of-Speech is also widely used by us in our writings.

PUN

A Pun consists in the use of a word in such a way

that it is capable of more than one application, the object being to introduce a ludicrous effect.

Examples:

— Is life worth living? It depends upon the liver.

In this sentence, the word 'liver' has been used in double meaning- the physical organ LIVER and the person who lives.

— An ambassador is an honest man who lies aboard for the good of his country.

In this sentence, the word 'lies' has been used in double meaning- being and making false statement. These Figures-of-Speech are widely used by us in our communications.

METONYMY

In Metonymy, (literally change of name) an object is designed by the name of something which is associated with it.

Examples:

— The Bench, for the Judges...

— The House, for the members of Parliament...

— The laurel, for success...

— The Crown, for the King...

Since there are many kinds of association between objects, there are several varieties of Metonymy.

Thus Metonymy may result from the use of:

The sign for the person or thing symbolized:

Examples:

— You must address the chair. (The Chairman)

— One should work hard from the cradle to the grave. (From infancy to death)

The container for the thing contained:

Examples:

— The whole city went out to see that victorious general.

— The kettle boils.

— Forthwith he drank the fatal cup.

— He keeps a good cellar.

— He was playing to the gallery.

— He has undoubtedly the best stable in the country.

These Figures-of-Speech are widely used by us in our communications.

The instrument for the agent:

Examples:

— The pen is mightier than the sword.

The author for his works:

Examples:

— We are reading Milton.

— Do you learn Euclid at your school?

These Figures-of-Speech are widely used by us in our communications.

SYNECDOCHE

In Synecdoche, a part is used to designate the whole or the whole to designate a part.

A part used to designate whole:

Examples:

- Give us this day our daily bread. (I.e. food)
- Uneasy lies the head that wears the crown.
- He has many mouths to feed.
- All the best brains could not solve the problem.

The whole used to designate a part:

Examples:

- England (i.e. the cricket team of England) won the first test match against Australia.

These Figures-of-Speech are widely used by us in our communications.

TRANSFERRED EPITHET

In this figure, an epithet is transformed from its proper word to another that is closely associated with that in the sentence.

Examples:

- He passed sleepless night.
- A lackey presented an obsequious cup of coffee.

LITOTES

In Litotes an affirmative is conveyed by negation of the opposite, the effect being to suggest a strong expression by means of a weaker. It is the opposite of Hyperbole.

Examples:

- I am a citizen of no mean. (I am a celebrated citizen)

— The man is no fool. (Very clever)

— I am not a little surprised. (Greatly)

These Figures-of-Speech are widely used by us in our communications.

INTERROGATION

Interrogation is asking of a question not for the sake of getting an answer, but to put a point more effectively.

Examples:

— Am I my brother's keeper?

— Who is here so vile that will not love his country?

EXCLAMATION

In this figure, the exclamatory form is used to draw greater attention to a point that mere bald statement of it could do.

Examples:

— What is piece of work is man!

— How sweet the moonlight sleeps upon this bank!

— what a fall was there, my countryman!

These Figures-of-Speech are widely used by us in our communications.

CLIMAX

Climax is the arrangement of a series of ideas in the order of increasing importance.

Examples:

— He is simple, erect, severe, austere and sublime.

- What a piece of work man! How noble in reason, how infinite in faculties! In action, how like an angel!
- In apprehension, how like a God!

ANTICLIMAX

Anticlimax is the opposite of Climax-a sudden descent from higher to lower. It is chiefly used for the purpose of satire or ridicule.

Examples:

- The great Dalhousie! The great god of war, you sometimes take counsel, and sometimes take tea.

These are the Figures-of-Speech that we usually use in our communications.

7

Being Fluent in English

Being fluent in English is important, considering it is the universal language of business communication. For those looking to improve their skills, here are a few tips.

LISTEN AND OBSERVE

As a baby, you began learning your mother tongue simply by listening and observing. This is the most natural method of learning a language. If you think grammar and rules of syntax bog you down, go back to the primal mode of learning—listen and observe. Be alert when you listen to someone speaking English, be it at your workplace, at a party or on television. Watch out for common expressions and usages. If you are able to grasp regularly used ways of greeting and small talk, you will be able to initiate speaking more confidently. Start noting simple things: If you meet someone at a party, do you always end up saying, 'Hi! Nice meeting you...'?

How about introducing variations here? Observe how others talk and try varying your greeting. Why not try saying 'How do you do?' or 'How are you doing?' Greetings and introduction lines may seem trivial, but if you are not fluent in a language, you often tend to avoid even these, thus ending all prospects of communication. If you can break this barrier, you can take your first step into the realm of English speaking.

READING SKILLS

While listening to English speakers definitely helps, it is important to read if you wish to expedite the process of improving. Most people are put off by this because they associate reading with big, literary books. However, what we are talking about is reading anything and everything written in correct English. Therefore, your range of choices could extend from comic strips to newspaper articles, gadget manuals to movie reviews. While reading, try and get a feel of the language and usage of words. More importantly, note the use of articles (a, an, the) and prepositions (in, on, at, from, into, over, under, etc) as these are areas where the most common errors are committed.

IMPROVE YOUR VOCABULARY

We are not asking you to learn the dictionary by rote! Can you commit yourself to learning two new words a day? You could come across these anywhere—while reading, on a news channel, on a sign at the shopping mall, on a billboard, etc. Make the effort to look up the exact meaning of the word in the dictionary, instead of adopting the easier route of understanding the meaning from the context.

If possible, maintain a book where you can note down the new words everyday, along with the context, so you remember them better. Write down the dictionary meaning and also frame a sentence using the word, so it is now registered in your memory.

PREPARE FOR SMALL TALK

Speaking English fluently is not just about making corporate presentations and giving long speeches. It is about expressing your views on the most mundane of things. How often do you meet a new person and face an awkward silence after the initial greeting because you don't know what to talk about? Worse, you may wish to initiate a conversation but may not be confident of putting something across correctly.

The ability to make small talk is very important in business and social conversations. Topics for casual conversation could include the weather, sports, current affairs, arts, hobbies, travel, etc. Read up on your area of interest and try framing sentences expressing your opinions. Talk about it with someone close to you so you can check for grammatical accuracy. Then, gradually build up on your repertoire of conversational topics and start using them whenever you get a chance. Of course, when you talk, do not make it sound like a speech you have learnt by heart. Induce a casual tone and adapt to the occasion.

Speak English with Body Language

Speak English with Body Language. When we speak, we use much more than just words. We also communicate with our face, our hands and even our own body. This kind of communication can be called Body Language or Non-Verbal Communication. Non-Verbal Communication not only includes how we move our body, but also hand gestures, facial expressions including eye contact and how we use our voice. Psychologists estimate that between 60% and 80% of all of our communication with other people is non-verbal. We communicate a wide range of information non-verbally. We also show our feelings, attitudes, moods, hopes and wishes far better with non-verbal language than with words.

Not only is a large Quantity of communication non-verbal in nature, but the Quality of Body Language is high as well. For example, if a person says something positive while his face looks negative, which are we more likely to believe? In most cases, we will believe the non-verbal facial expression. In the end, his words will not succeed in communicating his message. If we want to succeed in our everyday conversations, we really must learn to speak with our body well!

The main thing is to relax and be natural. Trying too hard to use Body Language will make you seem a bit strange. Instead, you should allow your body language to naturally follow your words. If you say something positive, then your face, body and hands should show it too. If you are expressing a sad or worried feeling, then your face, body and hands should change with that feeling. As you think about it more and consider how you can use your body to communicate, you will become more and more natural.

More specifically, let's talk about hand gestures. Using our hands, we can emphasize our main points, remind our listener how many main points we have and let our listener know when we are changing topics. A dramatic movement of the hand or moving our hands wide apart can signal how important something is. We can even use two fingers, either close together or far apart, to show how big something is. To show VERY strong feeling we could clap our hands together loudly or make a fist (put our fingers in a ball as though we want to hit someone) and hit a table or desk. To show that we welcome someone, on the other hand, we can hold our hands out with the palms up and maybe move them towards a chair to invite someone to sit next to us.

Of course, we can also use our fingers to count, but be careful. People in some countries do not count the same way as in China. In France, for example, people do not count ONE by holding up their first finger, called the index finger. Instead, they hold up their thumb. In Japan, some people put their thumb Down (with the four fingers up) to mean ONE! This can create confusion sometimes, so be sure not to use only non-verbal communication. Use words too, so that your listener will be sure to understand you.

Some hand gestures that are popular are waving to someone as a greeting or holding your index finger and thumb into a circle to mean OKAY. However, there are some countries where these can have bad meanings! It's important to be careful when using certain common gestures. Don't assume that everyone in the world understands one gesture in the same way. Still, you can use basic gestures most of the time and then when you see a strange reaction from your listener, you can make sure to emphasize your real meaning by using words and a different hand movement.

Facial expressions are a very common way that we use to communicate every day. When speaking English, it's generally good to smile at your listener from time to time, especially when he or she has made an interesting comment. Also nod your head up and down to show you are really interested. From time to time, you can add a sound of agreement, such as UH HUH or even just MMMM to show you are listening. Above all, it is important to maintain eye contact while listening. Sometimes it is okay to move your eyes away when you are speaking, because you do have to think about what you want to say. However the listener should almost always look at the speaker without moving the eyes away (without averting the eyes).

If you are speaking to someone while standing, it is important to stand neither too close nor too far from the speaker. Stand at a position that is comfortable for both of you. Again, though, you must be careful when talking to people from different countries. People from some southern European countries, such as France or Spain, often stand closer together when speaking than do Chinese people. And people from Arab countries such as Saudi Arabia stand even closer! You do not always have to adapt your behaviour when you meet people from around the world, but you should be aware of potential misunderstandings.

If, instead of standing, you are speaking to someone while talking, you can show your friendliness and Openness by leaning a little bit toward the speaker. Try to avoid folding your arms in front of your chest. Many people consider folding your arms as a cold Protective gesture. Instead, you could have your hands on your knees or one hand on your knee and the other at your side. You can fold your arms sometimes if you wish, but don't hold them there for a long time. As long as your hands move from time to time, the listener will not think that you are unfriendly.

Besides all of the obvious physical ways to communicate non-verbally, we have our voice. We use Intonation, Loudness and Pitch (how high or low our voice sounds) to change our meaning. Even when our voice does not make an actual word, it still can communicate feeling and attitude. Combined with the words we use, our voice can be a very powerful way to express what we mean.

— A strong voice can communicate confidence.

— A quiet voice communicates intimacy or some secret message.

— A loud, high pitched voice (similar to a girl screaming) can communicate nervousness or excitement.

— A deep voice might mean we are tired or not enthusiastic.

Body language is one of the basic skills that all students need.

MAKE MISTAKES

Can you learn swimming by standing at the edge of the pool? You have to take the plunge, right? It is the same with language. Unless you use the language, you will never know how good you are at it. Ask a few people close to you who are good at English to help. Make them interrupt you whenever you make a mistake and ask them to correct you. Be open to feedback. Do not be embarrassed to make mistakes, for that is the only way you will learn. That is how the process of acquiring fluency in a language occurs. As a child, you may have made a lot of mistakes before getting a good grasp of your mother tongue. The only difference now is that you are conscious of the mistakes.

Books on grammar are a good supplement to strengthen your command over the language. Finally, all you need is a will to learn and the initiative to begin. That done, it is simply a matter of time and effort!

Reputed Software Company is all geared up for a client visit. The clients have indicated that, after inspecting the progress of the project they have outsourced, they would like to meet the team members working on it.

Why? To select one team member for a stint onsite —something almost every software engineer aspires for. Ravi has been one of the most active members in the project and has done a wonderful job. He is technically brilliant, but has some concerns:

— Will he able to communicate his performance to the client in an impressive manner so that he is chosen?

— Why do his team mates not prefer to come to him for solutions and go to less capable people instead?

— His project manager doesn't seem to be very warm towards him either, although he does drop in those occasional mails appreciating his work.

Here is a typical scenario in an IT company; or for that matter, any organisation where interpersonal communication is involved. Or, like in Ravi's case, where an employee suffers from a lack of interpersonal skills.

TECHNICAL AND JOB-RELATED SKILLS

Technical and job-related skills are a must, but they are NOT sufficient when it comes to progressing up the ladder. With the traditional paternalistic style of leadership becoming passe, professional managers expect their teams to be proactive and communicate openly.

"Soft skills are very important in business. It is essential to be technically sound, but one should also have the ability to convey the idea to the masses in the simplest possible manner," says Mayurkumar Gadewar, an ERP consultant with Price waterhouse Coopers. With the boom in out sourcing taking root across industries, many professionals and subject matter experts directly deal with their clients on a regular basis. Their approachability and people skills are what ultimately sustain the contract their employers have bagged. "Planning is necessary but execution is also equally important. And it takes soft skills to execute any idea because it involves dealing with people directly," says Gadewar.

SOFT SKILLS

Behavioural training experts say there are several soft skills are required in these circumstances. Some of them include:

i. Interpersonal skills
ii. Team spirit
iii. Social grace
iv. Business etiquette
v. Negotiation skills
vi. Behavioural traits such as attitude, motivation and time management

Do you have these? If your answer is yes, good for you. But if your answer is no, then you know it is time to develop these skills.

Formal Training

There is a lot of argument in the industry as to whether it is possible to enhance soft skills in a few hours of training, especially when one considers the fact that a person has lived with those traits all his life. To this, the answer is harsh but real -- a professional who wants to do well in his/ her career does not really have a choice. In the initial years of your career, your technical abilities are important to get good assignments. However, when it comes to growing in an organisation, it is your personality that matters, more so in large organisations where several people with similar technical expertise will compete for a promotion. Training on soft skills becomes all the more relevant in a country where the education system does not delve into personality development.

"Soft skills' training is essential because we do not have it in our academic curricula. Therefore, corporate houses have to take up the task of grooming employees who are the link between the company and the external world, so that they are able to present themselves better, " says Summit Mehta, an equity research analyst with Fortis Securities Ltd.

Be your Own Trainer!

While organisations are definitely investing in augmenting their staff's people skills, here are some inputs for professionals and students who would like to initiate the process themselves:

i. *Be a part of team activities*: It could be either as a part of your church choir, or an NGO, or your local youth circle. Observe your own behaviour in the group and how you relate to others.

ii. *Ask family members or close friends to write down your best and worst traits*. Ideally, have at least four to five people do this for you. Evaluate the common traits all of them have mentioned.

Thus, you can be aware of your strengths and work improving your weaknesses.

iii. *How well do you manage your time?* Think. Can you do more in life? Or is your day too crammed with activities? Effective time management is very essential in the corporate world.

iv. *Introspect on how you react to feedback.* In organisations, people skills mostly come into the picture when there is feedback given—be it for an idea, an executed project or a presentation.

You are judged by the way you respond to feedback. Do you get defensive? Do you insist you were right? Do you meekly accept criticism? Remember, people tend to be judged and stereotyped according to their responses. You will, too.

v. *How good are you at critiquing?,* While responding to feedback is one side of the coin, giving feedback is the other side. Are you aggressive? Pessimistic? Do you believe in constructive criticism? Or prefer to be the yes-man?

vi. *Live consciously,* Any organisation is manned by people, therefore soft skills are all about how you deal with people and present yourself.

Though it may be easier said than done, soft skills can be enhanced simply by being aware of oneself and living consciously.

Etiquette and polish, both in personal and business settings, are linked to how well we communicate.

Most people think communication is all about speaking and devalue the importance of listening. And many others don't realise what a vast difference there is between simply hearing what is being said and really listening. People who know how to listen learn more, care more, and end up being the ones we want to be around socially as well as professionally.

IMPROVE LISTENING SKILLS

Understand why you need to listen and remember to practise these tips the next time you conduct a conversation. Your eyes are a ead giveaway if you are not listening. When your mind wanders and you begin thinking of something or someone else, your eyes show your disinterest. And the person speaking to you is well aware that you are not paying attention. And this is true even if you don't look away. Blank stares don't conceal boredom!

Have you been wondering how to put together impressively-phrased Powerpoint presentation? Have you been wondering how to compose an e-mail that captures your strategies and goals effectively? It is time you did something about it. As a young professional in today's global business world, it is imperative that you are competent in both oral as well as written communication.

Forming Good Habits

Good and bad habits, once formed, are difficult to undo. It is hoped that the things which you learn in connection with reading, speaking and pronouncing English will be correct, because psychologists tell us that if you do a thing a certain way three times in succession, a habit will be formed which will be difficult to undo. After all, we may be intellectually superior to other animal species, but we are basically animals and you will find that if you are training a dog, cat, horse etc, the same principles will apply.

Perhaps you may give your pet dog a treat if they have done something the way you want them to do it three times, but usually, after that they will continue using the habit which they have now acquired without even thinking about it.

Forms of Oral Communication

- Building interpersonal relationships.
- Giving presentations and debating viewpoints effectively. You need to master oral skills for both in-person and over-the-phone interactions.

Similarly, important written communication includes:

- Writing professional e-mails (sans SMS slang).
- Putting together concise reports.
- Creating visually powerful Powerpoint presentations.

And the key to acing oral and written communication is to spruce up your communication skills. And it is a lot easier than you think.

Here are some easy tips to do it on your own:

1. *Improve pronunciation and diction:* There are a few tricks to making a vernacular accent more globally understandable.
   - Try making sure that 'air' comes out of your mouth when saying the letters, 'T, P, K' and the sound 'Ch'.
   - Focus on elongating your vowel sounds. This will also automatically slow down your rate of speech.
   - Sing English songs out loud!
   - Watch news shows on channels like CNN and BBC.

2. *Spruce up your writing skills*
   - Believe it or not, you have to Read More!
   - Well-written magazines, like The Economist and India Today, are great to read not only to improve language skills but also to learn more about the world.
   - In terms of books, read what interests you. The basic goal is to read as much as you can.

There are a plethora of good authors who are popular today. Some good writers whose language is easy to follow include Vikram Seth, Jhumpa Lahiri, Paulo Coelho, J D Salinger, Albert Camus and Roald Dahl.

   - People tend to forget basic grammar when writing e-mails. An e-mail is nothing more than a letter which is sent electronically.

Make sure salutations and content are professional. Use special phrases when attaching documents. For example, "Please find attached with this e-mail a report on..." This helps you sound professional.

3. Five exercises to practise every day!
   1. Pretend you are a newscaster and read out the newspaper to your mirror.
   2. Do not read local newspapers. Focus on national newspapers.
   3. While reading a book, underline all the words you do not know. Look them up in the dictionary.
   4. Make a list of these words, and make sure you use at least five of them in a conversation during the day.

v. Most important, make an effort to speak in English to your friends and family.

Many deserving candidates lose out on job opportunities because of their vernacular accent.

Can I 'Neutralise' my Accent?

Yes, you can. All you need to do is train yourself to speak English as comfortably and perfectly as you speak your mother tongue. How do you train yourself? By inculcating certain practices in your daily lifestyle. These will get you closer to sounding like a native English speaker and equip you with a global accent—and you will speak not American or British English, but correct English.

This is the first step to learn any other accent, be it American or British or Australian. Lisa Mojsin, head trainer, director and founder of the Accurate English Training Company in Los Angeles, offers these tips to help 'neutralise' your accent or rather do away with the local twang, as you speak.

i. *Observe the mouth movements of those who speak English well and try to imitate them*: When you are watching television, observe the mouth movements of the speakers. Repeat what they are saying, while imitating the intonation and rhythm of their speech.

ii. *Until you learn the correct intonation and rhythm of English, slow your speech down:* If you speak too quickly, and with the wrong intonation and rhythm, native speakers will have a hard time understanding you. Don't worry about your listener getting impatient with your slow speech -- it is more important that everything you say be understood.

iii. *Listen to the 'music' of English:* Do not use the 'music' of your native language when you speak English. Each language has its own way of 'singing'.

iv. *Use the dictionary*: Try and familiarise yourself with the phonetic symbols of your dictionary. Look up the correct pronunciation of words that are hard for you to say.

v. *Make a list of frequently used words that you find difficult to pronounce and ask someone who speaks the language well to pronounce them for you:* Record these words, listen to them and practice saying them. Listen and read at the same time.

vi. *Buy books on tape:* Compare the sound of your English with that of the person reading the book on the tape.

vii. *Pronounce the ending of each word:* Pay special attention to 'S' and 'ED' endings. This will help you strengthen the mouth muscles that you use when you speak English.

viii. *Read aloud in English for 15-20 minutes every day:* Research has shown it takes about three months of daily practice to develop strong mouth muscles for speaking a new language.

ix. *Record your own voice and listen for pronunciation mistakes*: Many people hate to hear the sound of their voice and avoid listening to themselves speak. However, this is a very important exercise because doing it will help you become conscious of the mistakes you are making.

x. *Be patient*: You can change the way you speak but it won't happen overnight. People often expect instant results and give up too soon. You can change the way you sound if you are willing to put some effort into it.

MOST DIFFICULT LANGUAGE

We are often asked what is the most difficult language to learn and it is a difficult question to answer because there are a lot of things to take into consideration. Firstly, as a first language or mother tongue, the differences are unimportant, so the question of how hard a language is to learn only arises in the area of second language acquisition.

A native speaker of Spanish will find Portuguese much easier to learn than a native speaker of Chinese, for example, because Portuguese is very similar to Spanish, while Chinese is very different, so first language is an important factor. The more different a language is from our mother tongue, the harder it will be to learn. Many people answer that Chinese is the hardest language to learn, possibly influenced by the thought of learning Chinese characters and the pronunciation of Chinese does appear to be very difficult for foreign learners. However, for Japanese speakers, who already use Chinese characters in their own language, the writing will be less of a challenge than it will for people from languages using the Roman alphabet.

Some people can learn languages naturally and easily without much effort, while others find it very difficult, so natural aptitude for language learning is another factor. Teachers and the circumstances in which we learn also play an important role as well as the motivation for learning. If people learn a language they need to use, they often learn it faster than people studying a language that has no direct use in the lives.

There is no single answer to this question: What is the most difficult language to learn?. It depends on so many factors. However, the British Foreign

Office has looked at the languages that diplomats and other embassy staff have to learn and has worked out which they find the most difficult to learn.

The second hardest is Japanese which probably comes as no surprise to many, but the language that they have found to be the most difficult to learn is Hungarian which has 35 cases (forms of a nouns according to whether it is subject, object, genitive, etc). This does not mean that Hungarian is the hardest language to learn for everybody, but it causes British diplomatic staff, who are used to learning languages, the most difficulty. However, Tabassaran, a Caucasian language has 48 cases, so it would probably cause more difficulty if British diplomats had to learn it.

Different cultures and individuals from those cultures will find different languages more difficult. In the case of Hungarian for British learners, it is not a question of the writing system, which is alphabetic, but the grammatical complexity, though native speakers of related languages may find it easier, while struggling with languages that we find relatively easy. No language is easy to learn well, though languages which are related to our first language will be easier. Learning a completely different writing system is a huge challenge, but that does not necessarily make a language more difficult that another. In the end, it is impossible to say that there is one language that is the most difficult language in the world.

70 WAYS TO IMPROVE YOUR ENGLISH

Here is The List of 70 Ways to Improve Your English.

1. *Start your own English Language Blog*: Even for people who don't have to write in English, writing can be a great way of properly learning the kind of vocabulary. You need to describe your own life and interests, and of thinking about how to stop making grammar mistakes. The problem most people have is that they don't know what to write about. One traditional way to make sure you write every day in English is to write an English diary (journal) and a more up to date way of doing this is to write a blog. Popular topics include your language learning experience, your experience studying abroad, your local area, your language or translations of your local news into English.
2. *Write a news diary*: Another daily writing task that can work for people who would be bored by writing about their own routines in a diary is to write about the news that you read and listen to everyday. If you include your predictions for how you think the story will develop (e.g. "I think Hillary will become president"), this can give you a good reason to read old entries another time, at which time you can also correct and mistakes you have made and generally improve what you have written.
3. *Sign up for a regular English tip*: Some websites offer a weekly or even daily short English lesson sent to your e-mail account. If your mobile phone has an e-mail address, it is also possible to have the tips sent to your phone to read on the way to work or school. Please note, however, that such services are not usually graded very well to the levels of different students and they should be used as a little

added extra or revision in your English studies rather than as a replacement for something you or your teacher have chosen more carefully as what you need to learn.

4. *Listen to MP3s*: Although buying music on the internet is becoming more popular in many countries, not so many people know that you can download speech radio such as audio books (an actor reading out a novel) and speech radio. Not only is this better practice for your English than listening to English music, from sources like Scientific American, BBC and Australia's ABC Radio it is also free.

5. *Listen to English Music:* Even listening to music while doing something else can help a little for things like getting used to the natural rhythm and tone of English speech, although the more time and attention you give to a song the more you will learn from listening to it again in the future.

6. *Read the lyrics to a song*: Although just listening to a song in English can be a good way of really learning the words of the chorus in an easily memorable way, if you want to really get something out of listening to English music you will need to take some time to read the lyrics of the song with a dictionary. If the lyrics are not given in the CD booklet, you may be able to find them on the internet, but please note that some lyrics sites deliberately put a few errors into their lyrics for copyright reasons. Once you have read and understood the lyrics, if you then listen and read at the same time, this can be a good way of understanding how sounds change in fast, natural, informal speech.

7. *Sing karaoke in English*: The next stage after understanding and memorising a song is obviously to sing it. Although some words have their pronunciation changed completely to fit in with a song, most of the words have the same sounds and stressed syllables as in normal speech. Remembering which words rhyme at the end of each line can also be a good way of starting to learn English pronunciation.
8. *Write a film, music, hotel or book review*: Another motivating and easy way to make yourself write in English is to write a review for a site such as Amazon or Internet Movie Database. Many non-native speakers write reviews on sites like this and if you have some special understanding of the book, music or film due to your first language or knowing the artist personally, that would be very interesting for the English speakers who read and write reviews on the site.
9. *Only search in English:* Switching your search engine to the English language version of msn, yahoo, Google etc. can not only be a good way of practising fast reading for specific information in English, but could also give you a wider choice of sites to choose from and give you an idea of what foreigners are writing about your country and area.
10. *Read a book you've already read or seen the movie of in your own language*: Although most language learners under Advanced level would probably learn more from reading a graded reader or something from the internet than they would from reading an original book written for English speakers, for some people reading something like Harry Potter in the original can

be a great motivator to improve their English. To make this easier for you and make sure that it motivates you rather than just making your tired, try reading a book that you already know the story of. This not only makes it easier to understand and guess vocabulary, but you are also more likely to remember the language in it. If you have not read the book before, reading a plot summary from the internet can also help in the same way.

11. *Read a translation into English*: Another way of making sure books are easier to understand is to choose a book that was originally translated into English, preferably from your own language. Even if you haven't read the book in your own language, you will find the English is written in a slightly simplified way that is more similar to how your own language is written than a book originally written in English would be.
12. *Skip the first ten pages*: If you have given up with a book in English or are reading it very slowly, try skimming through the first ten pages or skipping them completely. The start of most books tend to be mainly description and are therefore full of difficult vocabulary and don't have a clear story line yet to help you understand what is happening and to motivate you to turn the next page. If the book is still too difficult even after the introductionary part is finished, it is probably time to give that book up for now and try it again after you have read some easier things.
13. *Read a book with lots of dialogue*: Opening up books before you buy one and flicking through them to find one with lots of direct dialogue in it has several advantages. If there is less text on

the page due to all the speech marks etc, this can make it easier to read and easier to write translations on. Dialogue is also much easier to understand than descriptive parts of a book, and is much more like the language you will want to learn in order to be able to speak English.

14. *Read English language comics*: Even more than books with lots of dialogue, comics can be easy to understand and full of idiomatic language as it is actually spoken. There can be difficulties with slang, difficult to understand jokes and/ or dialogue written how people speak rather than with normal spellings, so try to choose which comic carefully. Usually, serious or adventure comics are easier to understand than funny ones.

15. *Read English language entertainment guides:* Nowadays most big cities in the world have an English language magazine and/ or on-line guide to the movies, plays, exhibitions that are on in the city that week. Reading this in English is not only good value, but it could also guide you to places that English speakers are interested in and where you might hear some English spoken around you.

16. *Read English language magazines*: Like books, if you can read two versions of the same magazine (Newsweek in your language and in English, for example), that could make understanding it much easier.

17. *Take a one week intensive course:* Although you cannot expect to come out of a very short course speaking much better English than when you started it, if you continue studying a little over the following weeks and months, the knowledge

you gained then will gradually come out and mean that your level of speaking, listening etc. are better than they would have been if you hadn't taken that course. This positive effect can still be true up to a year later.

18. *Follow your intensive course up with an extensive course:* The more time you can spend studying English the better, but studying periodic intensive courses with a few hours of study a week in between is probably better value for money than any other system as it gives your brain time to subconsciously learn and start using the new language you have learnt before you introduce the next new "chunk" of language.
19. *Supplement your group class with a one to one class:* Another good way to combine two different kinds of classes is to study both in a group class and one to one. Having a one to one teacher, even if just a couple of times a month, will mean that you can be taught exactly the language that you need, that you will have more time to speak, and that you can have as much error correction as you like.
20. *Supplement your one to one class with a group class:* The benefits of having a group class are often less clear to students, but they include the fact that you will learn to deal with several people speaking at once, have a chance to practice skills such as interrupting people, and will hear a range of different viewpoints and topics.
21. *Teach your children or friends some English:* Recent research has shown that elder children tend to be a couple of IQ points above their younger siblings, and the most likely reason is that

explaining things to their little brothers and sisters gives them an intellectual boost. In the same way, teaching someone lower level than you the English you already know is a great way of permanently fixing that knowledge in your own brain.

22. *Ask your company to start English lessons:* Even if you don't need to speak English at work, English lessons can be a fun and reasonably priced way for your company to spend their training budget in a popular way.
23. *Have English radio on in the background while you are doing your housework:* Even if you are not listening carefully, it will help you get a feel for natural English rhythm and intonation.
24. *Play English language learning games on your Nintendo DS:* Although such games can have quite random language and are unlikely to improve your ability to speak English on their own, the next time you hear or read the same language elsewhere it will be really fixed in your brain by the fact you have played a game with it in already. It is also a nice way of taking a break from your other English studies while also doing some English. To make sure it really is a break and to avoid wasting time learning language from the game that is not much used in daily life, don't bother writing down any new language you see in the game, but just try to learn it from playing the game again.
25. *Say or think what you are doing in English as you do your daily tasks:* As you are doing your chores, try creating sentences describing what you are doing, e.g. 'I am unscrewing the ketchup bottle cap'. This gets you used to thinking in English

without translating, and can be a good way of seeing what simple vocabulary that is around you everyday you don't know yet

26. *Watch English language films with English subtitles:* For people who can't understand a film without subtitles but find themselves not listening at all when reading subtitles in their own language, this should be the way of watching a film that you should aim for. If it is too difficult to watch the whole film this way, try watching the (usually important) first 10 or 15 minutes of the film with subtitles in your own language, switch to English subtitles after that, and only switch back to subtitles in your own language if you get totally lost following the story of the film.
27. *Watch films in your language with English subtitles:* If you are finding English films with English subtitles too difficult or you can't find English films with English subtitles in your local video shop, this is a good second best option. Looking for local films with English subtitles can also sometimes be a good sign of quality, as it means the producers of the film are expecting it to be popular internationally as well.
28. *Watch English films with subtitles in your language:* Again, this is not as good practice as English language films with English subtitles, but is more relaxing, can be easier to find suitable DVDs for, and is also possible with VHS.
29. *Watch the same film or TV episode over and over again:* This can not only save you money on DVDs, but will mean that you can really learn the language without having to study it. Some comedies can also get funnier the more you watch them, especially if you watch them with

no subtitles and so understand a little more each time you watch it.

30. *Be realistic about your level:* One thing that holds many language learners back is actually trying too hard and tackling something that their brain is not ready for yet. Checking your level with a level check test on the internet, by taking an English language test (FCE, CAE, IELTS, TOEIC, TOEFL etc.), or by taking a free trial level check and/ or lesson in a language school will help you find out what your level is and so choose suitable self-study materials.
31. *Be realistic about your reading level*: Most researchers agree that people learn most when reading something they understand almost all of. If there are one or two words per page that you have never seen before, that is about the right level. If there are three or more on every page, you should switch to something easier and come back later.
32. *Read graded readers (= easy readers)*: These are books that are especially written for language learners like you, e.g. Penguin Readers. Although it can be difficult to find something as interesting as things written in newspapers or on the internet, in terms of learning the language only people who need to read for their work or an exam usually gain more from reading things written for graded readers. Graded readers of classic books like Charles Dickens also have the benefit of giving you a lot of knowledge about the literature, and culture more generally, of English speaking countries in a short time.
33. *Read the whole thing with no help:* Although using a dictionary has been shown to help with both

short term and long term learning of vocabulary, the fact that using it slows reading down can stop some people reading in English at all. Reading a whole book quickly through just for pleasure from time to time will help you remember how fun reading in another language can be.

34. *Read and learn everything:* At the opposite extreme, it can be hard work but very satisfying to get to the end of a book knowing that you have learnt every word in it.
35. *Watching English children's films or TV programmes:* Although some of the vocabulary you can learn from things made for children can be a bit strange (lots of animal names and maybe animal noises, including baby names for things), the fact that not only the language but the structure of the story is simplified can make it an easy and motivating thing to watch. Like good language learning materials, the same language is also often repeated to make it memorable, and the use of catchy songs etc. can increase this positive effect on your memory.
36. *Read English children's books:* This is very similar to watching English children's movies, but with the added advantage of there being more illustrations than adult books, which both helps you to understand the story and makes the page brighter and more motivating to read.
37. *Keep a list of language to learn, e.g. a vocabulary list:* Even if you don't often find time to go though your vocab list and it keeps on building up, just the act of choosing which words you need to learn and writing them down on a special list can help you learn them.

38. *Go through your vocab list several times every day:* If ticking off words on a vocabulary list on the train to work is inconvenient or embarrassing for you, you can keep your list of words to learn as an entry in your electronic dictionary, as a mobile phone to do list or as a text file in your MP3 player (e.g. iPod). Although the time spent transferring the information between different formats like these may seem wasted, in fact any time you spend using the vocabulary like this will help you learn it.

39. *Convert your vocab list to English only:* One way to stop yourself translating and therefore increase your speed of comprehension and production is to learn all your vocabulary without the use of your own first language. Ways you can write a vocab list in only English include with synonyms (words with the same meaning, e.g. "tall" and "high"); with opposites ("high" and "low"); with pronunciation factors such as number of syllables (the number of beats, e.g. three for "de- ci- sion") and the word stress (the syllable that is pronounced louder and longer, e.g. the second syllable in "baNAna"); and gapped sentences.

40. *Cross out and delete;* Crossing out or deleting words, sentences or whole pages that you have learnt can be a great motivator, and save your list of things to learn becoming too big to handle.

41. *Throw everything away and start again:* One of the things that can put most people off learning is a stack of half finished books or a huge list vocabulary waiting to be learnt. Simply getting rid of all that and starting again with something

new from zero can be a great motivator and get your studies underway again.

42. *Label things in your house or office with post-its:* The easiest vocabulary to learn is the vocabulary of things you see and use everyday. If you can write the names of things around you on slips of paper and stick them on the real thing, this is a great way of learning useful vocabulary. If you can leave them there over the following days and weeks, this is a very easy way of revising the vocabulary until it is properly learnt.

43. *Label a drawing:* For people who can't put labels on real things, the next best option is to take a photo of a real place in your life like your office, print it out, and then draw lines to all of the things you can see in the picture and label them in English with the help of a dictionary. You can do the same thing with places you pass through everyday like the station. Because you will see the same thing again and again, it should be easy to really learn the words for those things.

44. *Keep a diary in English:* This is a popular method of making sure you use English everyday for people who don't often speak English and can't think of things to write about. The fact that you are writing about real things that have happened to you means that any words you look up in the dictionary will be vocabulary that is useful for you and easy to learn.

45. *On-line chat:* The closest thing to speaking for people who don't have the chance to speak English is on-line chat, as you have to think and respond quickly, and the language is short and informal just like speech.

46. *Listen to the radio news in English:* You can make this easier by reading the news in English first, or even just by reading or listening to the news in your own language.
47. *Read an English language newspaper:* Freebie newspapers like "Metro" in London are usually the easiest to understand, followed by mid-brow titles like "The Daily Express" or "The Daily Mail" in English. Popular newspapers like "The Sun" are more difficult because of the idiomatic, slangy use of language and the number of jokes in the headlines and articles.
48. *Write fiction in English, e.g. short stories:* For people who find writing a diary about things that happen to them everyday boring, the best thing is to let your imagination go and write about whatever comes into your head. The advantage of this is that if you can't think of how to say something in English, you can just change the story to something that is easier to explain. Perhaps the easiest way to start writing fiction in English is with a diary, changing any details you like to make it more interesting and adding more and more fantasy as the weeks go on.
49. *English language exercise videos:* This is quite similar to how babies learn, by listening, watching and copying. It is also good for your health!
50. *Learn a famous speech or poem in English by heart:* Although you may never hear or get the chance to say exactly that line, having one memorable example of an English grammatical form in your head can make it much easier to learn other examples of the same grammar as you hear them. It is also something you can practice over

and over without being as boring as grammatical drills.

51. *Get tipsy (= a little drunk) before speaking English.* This can not only improve your fluency while you are drinking, but can also improve your confidence in future days and weeks by showing you that you can communicate what you want to say.
52. *Use a dictionary while you are watching a movie:* Films often have the same words many times, so if you look up important words the first or second time you hear them, you should have learnt them by the end of the film. It is easier to use a dictionary if you watch with English subtitles.
53. *Learn and use the phonemic script:* Although there are many sounds in English, there are even more spellings. By learning the phonemic script and writing vocabulary down with it, you can both add another stage to your vocabulary learning that should help you learn it more thoroughly, and improve your pronunciation. It can also make things easier for you by stopping you trying to pronounce different spellings of the same pronunciation different ways.
54. *Learn some spelling rules:* Many people think that English spelling is random, but in fact most words follow some kind of rule, e.g. the "magic E" that changes the pronunciation of "mad" and "made".
55. *Record your own voice:* For people who don't have much or any correction of pronunciation from a teacher, recording yourself and listening back makes it easier to hear whether you are

really making the English sounds that you are trying to or not.

56. *Use computer pronunciation analysis:* Although most programmes that claim to tell you when you are pronouncing correctly or not don't actually do that, listening many times and seeing how your voice changes as you try to match the sounds and waveform given by a pronunciation CD ROM can be good practice and more motivating than just recording your own voice.
57. *Learn as many words as you can of one category, e.g. animal words:* Learning similar words together can both expand your overall vocabulary and make them easier to learn by forming links between the words in your brain.
58. *Take holidays abroad:* This is not only a good opportunity to speak English in situations where you really have to make yourself understood in order to live, but it is also a good motivator to study English seriously in the weeks and months before your trip. If possible, also try to use English even when you could use your own language, e.g. when you pick a guided tour of a museum or historic place or when you book a flight on the internet, and try to avoid package tours.
59. *Draw pictures of the words you want to learn:* Especially if you are artistic, this can be a better way of learning vocabulary than writing translations or example sentences.
60. *Find a foreign boyfriend or girlfriend:* No tips on how to do this here, but everyone agrees that getting or even just looking for a date in English

can be a great motivator to improve your language skills.

61. *Arrange a conversation exchange:* Swapping lessons and conversation with someone who wants to learn your language can be a good alternative for those who aren't looking for romance, or can sometimes lead onto dating for those who are!

62. *Sign up for an English language exam:* Even if you don't need to take an exam and don't want to or can't take a special course to study for it, paying to take an exam like TOEFL, TOEIC, IELTS or FCE can really motivate you take your English studies seriously.

63. *Model your accent on one particular actor:* E.g. try to speak like Robert De Niro. Students who say they want to sound more like a native speaker have the problem that native speakers don't sound all that much like each other. Choosing one model can make the task of improving your pronunciation more clear, and is quite fun. Doing an impression of that person also makes a good party trick.

64. *Use an English-English dictionary:* Trying to use a bilingual dictionary less and switching to a monolingual one can help you to stop translating in you head when you are speaking or listening, and other useful English vocabulary can come up while you are using the dictionary.

65. *Occasionally talk to or e-mail your friends in English:* Many people find this a bit false or embarrassing, but if you think of it as a study club and set a particular time and/ or place, it is no different from studying Maths together.

66. *Go to an English or Irish pub:* As well as having a menu in English and being a good way of finding out something about the culture of English speaking countries, you might also find there are free English language listings magazines, English language sports on the TV and/ or foreign people you can speak to.
67. *Buy a speaking electronic dictionary:* Although most electronic dictionaries are not as good as paper ones for the amount of information they give you about each word, some of them have the very useful function of saying the word with the correct pronunciation.
68. *Learn your electronic dictionary vocabulary list:* Most electronic dictionaries also have a button which you can push to see the last 30 or more words you looked up. By deleting words you decide are useless or you have already learnt from this list, you can use it as a "to do list" of words to learn that you can look at several times a day in the train etc.
69. *Switch operating system to English:* Changing the operating language of your mobile phone, video recorder etc. to English can be an easy way of making sure you use the language everyday.
70. *Set goals:*. Deciding how many hours you want to study, how many words you want to learn or what score you want to get in a test are all good ways of making sure you do extra study.

8

Effective Use of English

USING WISH IN ENGLISH

Wish + Infinitive

I wish to see the manager.

This is like 'I would like to see the manager', but is more insistent and stronger, though still polite.

Wish + Noun / Pronoun + Past Simple

I wish I had the time to do it.

This means either that I don't have the time now or that I won't have the time in the future to do it, depending on context:

I wish I were/was rich.

Here, the speaker regrets that they are not rich now. Note that with the verb 'be', you can either use the past simple or the past subjunctive.

I wish I were/was able to go to the meeting next week.

Here, the speaker is clearly talking about the future.

Wish + Noun / Pronoun + Past Perfect

I wish I hadn't said that.

Here, the speaker is talking about the past. They said something and now they regret it.

Wish + Noun / Pronoun + Would/Could

I wish I could speak German.

Here, the speaker cannot speak German, but it is possible to learn it, so it is not as impossible as the sentences above. It is imaginary, but wouldn't be impossible to change the situation. If the subject of the verb wish and the verb after it are the same, we use could.

I wish he wouldn't play his music so late at night.

Again, the situation is imaginary, but it would be possible for the other person to turn their music down. As the two subjects are different we use would. It is possible to use could when talking about someone not having the opportunity or ability: I wish he could come with us.

USE OF RATHER IN ENGLISH

Rather as an Adverb of Degree

- *Modifying an adjective:* The film was rather good.
- *Modifying an adverb:* It happened rather quickly.

  Eg:

1. It is stronger than fairly, but not as strong as very.
2. It can modify a noun, often coming before the article:
3. It's rather a problem.
4. It can modify some verbs: I rather like it.

To Express Preference

Rather than

Rather than is normally used to compare parallel structures:

— Let's take the train rather than the bus.

— Rather you than me!

— I decided to write rather than e-mail.

Would rather:

Would rather + infinitive without 'to':

I'd rather leave now.

Would rather + pronoun + past tense:

I'd rather he came early.

ALL AND WHOLE

All and Whole often have the same meaning, but they are used differently.

WITH THE DEFINITE ARTICLE

— All comes before the definite article: All the time

— Whole comes after the definite article: The whole time

With a Possessive Adjective

— All comes before a possessive adjective: All my life

— Whole comes after a possessive adjective: My whole life

With a Singular Noun

— Whole can only be used after a definite article: The whole country (not 'Whole country')

With Plural Nouns

They have different meanings:

— All exams were affected. = Every exam was affected.

— Whole exams were affected. = This doesn't mean that every exam was affected, but that some were affected completely.

ADJECTIVES AND ADVERBS

Here is a list of adjectives that end in -ly and sometimes get mistaken for adverbs:

— Beastly

— Brotherly

— Comely

— Costly

— Cowardly

— Daily (Can also be an adverb)

— Deadly

— Elderly
— Fatherly
— Fortnightly (Can also be an adverb)
— Friendly
— Gentlemanly
— Gentlewomanly
— Ghastly
— Ghostly
— Godly
— Goodly
— Holy
— Homely
— Humanly
— Kingly
— Leisurely
— Likely
— Lively
— Lonely
— Lovely
— Lowly
— Maidenly
— Manly
— Masterly
— Matronly
— Miserly
— Monthly (Can also be an adverb)
— Motherly
— Nightly

— Painterly
— Priestly
— Princely
— Saintly
— Scholarly
— Shapely
— Silly
— Sisterly
— Timely
— Ugly
— Ungainly
— Unruly
— Unsightly
— Unseemly
— Unworldly
— Weekly (Can also be an adverb)
— Womanly
— Worldly
— Yearly (Can also be an adverb)

HOMONYMS

Homonyms are words that sound the same when pronounced, but are spelled differently and have different meanings.

Example: Loose and lose

Many people make this mistake. They inevitably interchange the words loose and lose while writing.

Lose means to suffer a loss or defeat.

Thus, you would write:

— Correct: I don't want to lose you.

— Wrong: I don't want to loose you.

Loose means Not Firm or Not Fitting.

In this context, you would write,

— Correct: My shirt is loose.

— Wrong: My shirt is lose.

Here are many more homonyms which you have to know to write distinctively.

— *Cache:* Hidden storage, as in: Lost in the woods, we were happy to find a cache of food belonging to some hunters.

— *Cash:* Money paid at the time of purchase, as in: Will this be cash or charge?

— *Calendar:* Device for showing divisions of time, as in: Mark this date on your calendar.

— *Colander:* Strainer, as in: Use the colander to drain the noodles.

— *Callous:* Unfeeling, as in: Drinking and driving shows a callous disregard for life.

— *Callus:* Hard, thickened skin, as in: I have a callus on my finger from holding the pencil.

— *Canvas:* Durable cloth made from cotton, linen, or hemp, as in: This fine painting is oil on canvas.

— *Canvass:* Go around asking, as in: Canvass the neighbourhood to see if anyone saw the suspect.

— *Capital:*

(1) City where the seat of government of a state or country is located, as in: Washington, D.

C. is the capital of the United States of America.

(2) Upper case letter, as in: Writing in all capitals on the Internet is considered shouting, and is rude.

- *Capitol:* Building in which the US Congress meets, as in: When I visited Washington, DC, I toured the Capitol.
- *Carton:* Lightweight container or box, as in: Please send me one carton of printer cartridges.
- *Cartoon:* Drawing, often humorous, as in: Dilbert is a popular cartoon character.
- *Casual:* Informal, as in: For a picnic in the park, it's best to wear casual clothes.
- *Causal:* Relating to a cause, as in: The causal forces behind many diseases have not been discovered yet.
- *Cease:* Stop, as in: If someone violates your copyright, send them a Cease and Desist letter immediately.
- *Seize:* Grab, as in: The guerillas tried to seize control of the town.
- *Siege:* Prolonged period of trouble or annoyance, as in: Our family has had a siege of bad colds this year.
- *Cede:* Yield, as in: At the war's end, the loser had to cede the disputed territory to the winner.
- *Seed:* Beginning of a new plant, as in: The seed of an avocado can be planted in soil or water.
- *Ceiling:* Upper limit of a room, as in: A light-coloured ceiling makes a room seem brighter.
- *Sealing:* Closing airtight, as in: Sealing the

containers is important to keep the contents fresh.

- *Cell:* Small room, as in: She will spend two months in a prison cell for her mistake.
- *Sell:* Offer for sale, as in: I will sell you my car.
- *Seller:* One who offers for sale, as in: Amazon.com is a seller of books.
- *Census:* Population count, as in: The last census showed an increase in single-parent families.
- *Senses:* Sound mental faculties, as in: Don't call me until you have come to your senses.
- *Cent:* One-hundredth of a monetary unit, as in: In the US, a penny is worth one cent.
- *Scent:* Odour, as in: The detective smelled the scent of almonds-could it be cyanide poisoning?
- *Sent:* Past tense of send, as in: I sent you E-mail yesterday.
- *Cents:* Plural of cent, as in: His opinion is only worth two cents.
- *Sense:* Method of perception, as in: Ears provide us with the sense of hearing.
- *Cereal:* Breakfast food prepared from grain, as in: My favourite cereal is Grape-Nuts; what's yours?
- *Serial:* Arranged in a series, as in: I hope they catch that serial killer soon.
- *Cession:* Act of ceding (surrendering) to another, as in: The treaty included cession of all captured territories.
- *Session:* Meeting or term, as in: I will take two classes during the summer session.

- *Choose:* Select, as in: There are many good programs to choose from.
- *Chose:* Past tense of choose, as in: My son chose a university near home.
- *Chic:* Stylishness and elegance: "Paris is the city for timeless bargain chic, in almost any category."
- *Chick:* Small chicken or bird: A chick pecks its way out of the egg.
- *Chord:* A combination of musical tones played simultaneously, as in: His symphony is entitled The Lost Chord.
- *Cord:* Small rope, as in: Please pull the silver cord to summon the maid.
- *Chute:* Slanted shaft from a higher level to a lower one, as in: The gravel came rumbling down the chute.
- *Shoot:* To discharge a weapon, as in: Don't shoot! I'm unarmed.
- *Cite:* Quote, as in: Your proposal will be more persuasive if you cite results of a recent survey.
- *Sight:* Vision, as in: Our eyes provide us with one sense of sight; our imagination, another.
- *Site:* Exact location, as in: Thank you for visiting my web site. Please come back often.
- *Cliche:* Overused expression, as in: A good business writer tries to avoid using a cliche.
- *Click:* Make a light, sharp sound, as in: The instructions said to click on the left mouse button.
- *Clique:* Small, exclusive group of people, as in: I wasn't invited to join their clique.

- *Climactic:* Having to do with the climax of something, as in: The villain falling off the cliff was the climactic scene of the movie.
- *Climatic:* Having to do with climate, as in: The climatic conditions in the South Pole can be described in one word: cold!
- *Close:* Shut, as in: Please close the door when you leave.
- *Clothes:* Wearing apparel, as in: Wear your nicest business clothes for your interview for that job.
- *Cloths:* Pieces of fabric, as in: Use the cloths under the sink for dusting.
- *Course:* Rough, as in: Their garments were made of a coarse cloth.
- *Course:*
  (1) Natural development, as in: The doctor said the disease must run its course.
  (2) A unit of study, as in: She got an A in that course.
- *Collision:* Crash, as in: Was anyone hurt in the collision?
- *Collusion:* Conspiracy, as in: The price rise was due to collusion among the manufacturers.
- *Coma:* Unconscious state, as in: The accident victim was in a coma for six months.
- *Comma:* Punctuation mark, as in: Use a comma to show where you would normally pause if you were reading the sentence out loud.
- *Command:* Give an order, as in: That sounded more like a command than a request.
- *Commend:* Praise, as in: I commend you for the effort in reading this list.

- *Commence:* Begin, as in: We commence work Monday at 9 A.M.
- *Comments:* Remarks, as in: I appreciate your comments about this list.
- *Complement:* That which completes, as in: As an author, I need input from readers to complement my point of view.
- *Compliment:* Expression of praise, as in: Sometimes a critical remark is more useful than a compliment.
- *Comprehensible:* Understandable, as in: I was surprised that the instructions were so comprehensible.
- *Comprehensive:* Covering a wide area, as in: In order to graduate, one must take a comprehensive examination of the subject.
- *Confidant:* Someone you tell secrets to, as in: He was always my best friend and confidant.
- *Confident:* Self-assured, as in: Are you confident you can finish the project on schedule?
- *Confidentially:* Spoken in a private manner, as in: Confidentially, I am looking for another job.
- *Confidently:* Firmly assured, as in: You can confidently raise your arms in public if you use a CERTAIN brand of deodorant, according to their television commercial.
- *Conscience:* Inner sense of right and wrong, as in: Wouldn't it bother your conscience to lie to your friends?
- *Conscious:* Aware or awake, as in: The patient was conscious for an hour, then relapsed into a coma.

– *Conservation:* Protection from loss or waste, as in: We show concern about conservation of bandwidth by making efficient Web pages.

– *Conversation:* Talk between people, as in: I very much enjoyed our conversation yesterday.

– *Consul:* Representative of a foreign government, as in: For our next seminar about exporting, let's see if we can get a consul from an Eastern European country to be a featured speaker.

– *Council:* Elected or appointed group of people assembled for governing or advising, as in: We're going to have to take that idea up with the town council.

– *Counsel:*

(1). Give advice or opinion, as in: Volunteers counsel the young people.

(2) Attorney, as in: I had this contract drawn up on advice of counsel.

– *Consular:* Having to do with the representative of a foreign government, as in: Phone Wieslaw Czyzowicz, the man in charge of consular affairs at the Polish Consulate.

– *Councillor:* Appointed or elected member of a council, as in: As councilor for this township, I welcome your ideas.

– *Counselor:* Advisor, as in: You need a letter from your guidance counselor for your scholarship application.

– *Continual:* Occurring frequently and regularly, as in: Every night we are disturbed by the continual barking of your dog.

– *Continuous:* Unbroken, as in: He writes his name in one long, continuous line.

- *Contiguous:* Adjacent or touching, as in: The contiguous states of the United States do not include Alaska and Hawaii.
- *Cooperation:* Work together for a common purpose, as in: Many people believe cooperation will help you succeed more than competition will.
- *Corporation:* A business structure, as in: A corporation is established by the authority of a state government and exists independent of the people who own it.
- *Core:* Central or essential part, as in: A good communicator emphasizes the core of the message.
- *Corps:* A group of people who act as a body rather than as individuals, as in: She was satisfied to dance with the corps de ballet rather to become a soloist.
- *Corespondents:* Joint defendants in a court case, as in: The bank official and his secretary were corespondents in the divorce trial.
- *Correspondence:* Exchange of letters, as in: I'm so busy with work it's hard to keep up with my correspondence.
- *Costume:* Specialised style of dress, as in: I wore a peasant costume to the Renaissance Fair.
- *Custom:* Habitual practice, as in: In the United States, business people have the custom of shaking hands when they meet.
- *Courtesy:* Politeness, as in: Your staff extended me every courtesy during my stay at your hotel.
- *Curtsy:* Bow with bended knees, as in: When a woman is presented to the Queen, she is expected to curtsy.

- *Credible:* Believable, as in: Unfortunately, we don't have a credible witness to the crime.
- *Creditable:* Praiseworthy, as in: He did a creditable job in winning us that contract.
- *Critic:* One who evaluates, as in: The critic gave the new movie a favorable review.
- *Critique:* A formal analysis of a work, as in: Please send your request for a site review to the HWG critique mailing list.
- *Cue:* Signal to begin, as in: At the meeting, I won't say anything until I get the cue from you.
- *Queue:* People in line, as in: We had to wait in the queue to get tickets for the movie.
- *Currant:* A berry, as in: I made some fresh currant jam to go with the biscuits.
- *Current:* Up to date, as in: The current issue of Internet World has some good information on graphics design.
- *Dairy:* Having to do with milk and milk products, as in: Our best customer sells dairy products.
- Diary: Daily record of events, as in: I kept a diary when the twins were tiny, to help me remember which baby I fed last.
- *Data:* Facts and figures, as in: He designed a survey to collect data about visitors to his Web site.
- *Datum:* A single fact, as in: We based our measurements on the datum of the boiling point of water. (Note: rarely used outside scientific literature)
- *Deceased:* Dead, as in: I am sorry to report that

our hospital records show that your uncle is deceased.

- *Diseased:* Seriously ill: The fact that he was poor and diseased never seemed to affect his wonderful sense of humor.
- *Decent:* In good taste, as in: Gestures considered decent in one culture may be obscene in another.
- *Descent:* Going downward, as in: His descent from the airplane was much slower after he pulled the cord on his parachute.
- *Dissent:* Disagreement, as in: Of the twelve judges ruling on the case, hers was the only voice of dissent.
- *Dissidence:* Strong disagreement and outright opposition, as in: The government's oppressive policies led to such dissidence that they were ousted in the next election.
- *Decree:* Official decision or order, as in: The decree made all the striking workers return to their jobs.
- *Degree:* Step, grade, or rank, as in: She suffered third-degree burns on her arms rescuing the child.
- *Decry:* To openly condemn or ridicule, as in: Those who believe in a democratic society decry tyranny in any form.
- *Descry:* To see or catch sight of, often from a distance, as in: When I descry the island, I'll shout, "Land Ho!"
- *Deduce:* Form an opinion from a solid basis of fact, as in: From the size of these shoeprints, I deduce the intruder was wearing large shoes.

(You thought I was going to say had large feet, didn't you?)

- *Deduct:* Subtract, as in: Please deduct this amount from my bill.
- *Defer:*
  (1) Delay or postpone, as in: We can defer the charges one month.
  (2) Yield out of respect, as in: I defer to my colleague's greater experience in this field.
- *Differ:* Disagree, as in: I must differ with you about the meaning of that word.
- *Deference:* Courteous regard, as in: The young people in that family showed great deference for their elders.
- *Difference:* Distinguishing characteristic, as in: The difference is that my web site loads quickly while your's does not.
- *Delusion:* Mistaken belief of a confused state of mind, as in: He was under the delusion that he could fly.
- *Allusion:* Indirect or casual mention, as in: No one made any allusion to the scandal while she was in the room.
- *Elusion:* Evasion or clever escape, as in: The embezzlers celebrated their elusion of the police a little too soon.
- *Illusion:* Presentation of a false or misleading idea, as in: The magician gave the illusion of sawing the woman in half.
- *Deposition:* Sworn, written statement, as in: Before the start of the trial, each of the witnesses gave a deposition of their testimony.

— *Disposition:*
  (1) Tendency to react in a certain way, as in: Pollyanna had an especially cheerful disposition.
  (2) Final settlement, as in: The disposition of my father's estate took longer than I thought it would.

— *Depraved:* Extreme departure from what is normal and good, as in: He was a depraved murderer.

— *Deprived:* Take away from, as in: He claimed that, during his childhood, he was deprived of any warmth and affection.

— *Deprecate:* Belittle, as in: Have you noticed that he seems to deprecate himself just so we have to compliment him?

— *Depreciate:* Fall in value or price, as in: A new car will start to depreciate as soon as you drive it off the lot.

— *Desert:*
  (1) Hot, dry, sandy place, as in: Not all kinds of plants can grow in a desert.
  (2) Abandon or forsake, as in: The loyal little dog refused to desert his master.

— *Dessert:* End of a meal, usually something sweet, as in: I don't think I'll order any dessert today, thank you.

— *Desolate:*
  (1) Deserted or uninhabited, as in: They washed up on the shore of a desolate island.
  (2) Miserable, as in: I am desolate that you believed I could do a thing like that.

- *Dissolute:* Characterised by loose moral standards, as in: The younger son led a dissolute lifestyle before he returned home to his family.
- *Detract:* Take something away from the value or reputation of, as in: Words that are not properly used can detract from a writer's credibility.
- *Distract:* Divert attention from, as in: A blinking graphic on a Web page will distract a reader trying to read text.
- *Device:* Invention, as in: If your device works, I think you should get a patent for it.
- *Devise:* Think up a way to do something new, as in: HTML was devised to tell a Web browser how to show the relative importance of lines of text in a Web document.
- *Dew:* Moisture, as in: It was a beautiful spring morning, and the grass sparkled with dew.
- *Do:* Make, cause, perform, carry out, and act, as in: What shall I do to convince them?
- *Due:* Payable, as in: The rent is due the first of every month.
- *Die:*

  (1) Stop living or existing, as in: The doctor said without an operation the patient would surely die.

  (2) Device for shaping, as in: He used to be a tool-and-die maker before the terrible accident.
- *Dye:* Color, as in: I think I will dye my hair a lighter shade.
- *Disapprove:* View with disfavor, as in: His parents disapprove of his truancy.

- *Disprove:* Prove to be false, as in: The accused was determined to disprove the charges against him.
- *Disassemble:* Take apart, as in: It was easy to disassemble the clock, but it wasn't so easy to put it back together again.
- *Dissemble:* Disguise or conceal the real nature of, as in: I'd rather be honest about my shortcomings than dissemble or pretend to be something I'm not.
- *Disburse:* Pay out funds, as in: Do you think the foundation will disburse the funds soon?
- *Disperse:* Scatter, as in: The security guards told the crowd to disperse or face arrest.
- *Discreet:* Prudent, trustworthy, as in: A discreet accountant is a valuable business asset.
- *Discrete:* Separate and distinct, as in: The company is composed of three discrete units.
- *Disinterested:* Not influenced by personal motives, as in: To mediate this argument, we need a disinterested person.
- *Uninterested:* Unconcerned, as in: I knew she was sick because she was uninterested in food.
- *Divers:* Various, several, as in: We have provided divers acts for your entertainment.
- *Diverse:* Markedly different or conspicuously contrasting, as in: His hobbies are as diverse as whitewater-rafting and needlepoint.
- *Done:* Completed, as in: Call me when the Web site is done.
- *Dun:* Demand repeatedly, as in: The collection agency went to great lengths to dun him for payment of his.

- *Edition:* Published version, as in: Read the latest edition of the Tax Tips and Tactics newsletter.
- *Addition:* Something added, as in: We toured the addition to the hospital yesterday.
- *Effect:*
  - (1, a noun) immediate or direct result, as in: What effect does that medicine have on you?
  - (2, a verb) accomplish, as in: He braided the bedsheets to effect an escape.
- *Affect:* To act upon or influence, as in: Strong emotions can affect your health.
- *Effective:* Producing the desired result, as in: He has an effective introduction in his presentation.
- *Efficient:* Producing the desired result with the least waste, as in: I design graphics for Web pages that are an efficient use of bandwidth.
- *Eight:* The number after seven, as in: Breakfast will be at eight in the morning.
- *Ate:* Past tense of eat, as in: We ate in that new restaurant last week.
- *Elapse:* (Of time) pass by, as in: Three minutes elapsed before her page had completely loaded--too many graphics!
- *Lapse:*

  (1) To slip or fall, as in: When the announcement came, we all lapsed into silence.

  (2) To lose effect, as in: Your insurance policy will lapse if you don't pay the premiums.
- *Relapse:* A slip backwards, as in: Just when we thought he was going to get well, he suffered a relapse.

- *Elicit:* Draw out, as in: The band's performances always elicit praise from the critics.
- *Illicit:* Not allowed, as in: Illicit copying of another person's work is punishable by law.
- *Eligible:* Qualified for, as in: Every person who submits a new word this month is eligible to win the prize.
- *Illegible:* Hard to read, as in: I have seen Web sites where the text was illegible because the background was too strong a design.
- *Ineligible:* Legally disqualified, as in: In the US, a president who has been elected twice is ineligible to run again.
- *Allusion:* Indirect or casual mention, as in: No one made any allusion to the scandal while she was in the room.
- *Illusion:* Presentation of a false or misleading idea, as in: The magician gave the illusion of sawing the woman in half.
- *Delusion:* Mistaken belief of a confused state of mind, as in: He was under the delusion that he could fly.
- *Elusion:* Evasion or clever escape, as in: The embezzlers celebrated their elusion of the police a little too soon.
- *Elusive:* Hard to catch or grasp, as in: The solution to the problem proved more elusive than they first thought.
- *Illusive:* Deceptive or unreal, as in: Lost in the desert, he saw an illusive oasis called a mirage.
- *Emerge:* Come out of something enclosed, as in: Out of four candidates, you emerge as the favorite.

- *Immerge:* Plunge into (same as immerse), as in: Immerge the burn in cold water to minimize the skin damage.
- *Immerse:* Plunge into, as in: Sometimes we get so immersed in our work, we forget how much time has elapsed.
- *Emigrate:* Move out of a country, as in: My neighbors decided to emigrate to New Zealand [Images] while the children were still young.
- *Immigrate:* Move into a country, as in: My mother immigrated to this country from Lithuania.
- *Emanate:* Flow out from, as in: She was so creative that ideas just seemed to emanate from her.
- *Eminent:* Outstanding, as in: Steven Hawking is one of the most eminent thinkers of our time.
- *Imminent:* Impending, as in: When she heard a storm was imminent, she backed up her work and unplugged the computer.
- *En route:* On the way, as in: En route to town to sell the cow, Jack traded the cow for some magic beans.
- *Root:*
  (1) Underground part of a plant, as in: A carrot is a root vegetable.
  (2) Origin or source, as in: We can't solve this problem until we get to its root.
  (3) cheer for or wish success for, as in: Who did you root for in the Olympics ?
- *Rout:* Terrible defeat, as in: The Super Bowl turned out to be a complete rout.

- *Route:* A path which is planned and followed regularly, as in: I'm thinking of supplementing my salary with a newspaper route.
- Declare positively, as in: I assure you that I will be finished by next Tuesday.
- *Ensure:* Make sure, as in: Order today to ensure delivery by Monday.
- *Insure:* Cover by insurance, as in: This Company will insure the data on my hard disk as well as the computer itself.
- *Envelop:* Enfold or surround completely, as in: The python slithered forward to envelop its prey and crush it.
- *Envelope:* Container for a letter, as in: Please send a long, self-addressed, stamped envelope with your request.
- *Equable:* Even or equal and uniform, as in: Their goal is to create a more equable taxation system.
- *Equitable:* Fair and just, as in: The injured party sought an equitable settlement.
- *Erasable:* Capable of being rubbed out or removed, as in: Don't use an eraseable pen when doing your bookkeeping records, because these records are supposed to be permanent.
- *Irascible:* Easily provoked to anger, as in: After years of enduring chronic pain, he became so irascible it took courage to go visit him.
- *Especially:* Standing apart uniquely from the rest, as in: The air quality where I live is especially bad.
- *Specially:* Given unusual treatment, as in: Look in the specially-marked boxes for your entry blank.

– *Assay:* Chemical analysis, as in: The assay office will test your ore to see how much gold it contains.
– *Essay:* A short composition expressing the author's opinions, as in: Students applying for a scholarship often have to write an essay.
– *Every day:* Each day without exception, as in: Every day, he comes home and says, "Hi, Honey. What's for dinner?"
– *Everyday:* Ordinary, as in: Wear your everyday clothes to school, and save your finest for special occasions.
– *Every one:* Each, without exception, as in: I bought a dozen eggs yesterday and every one was cracked when I got home.
– *Everyone:* Everybody, as in: Everyone at work says to tell you, "Get well soon."
– *Ewe:* Female sheep, as in: The ewe was bleating and looking for her lamb.
– *Yew:* Evergreen tree of the taxus genus, as in: The finest violin bows are made of yew wood.
– *You:* The one or ones being spoken to, as in: I guarantee that you will be satisfied or your money will be cheerfully refunded.
– *Exalt:* Glorify or put much higher, as in: In ancient Egypt, the pharoah was exalted over his subjects.
– *Exult:* Rejoice, as in: The winning team went to the restaurant to exult in their victory.
– *ACCEDE:*

(1) Give in to, as in: We accede to your demands.

(2) take a position of authority, as in: When did the King accede to the throne?

- *Exceed:* To go past a stated amount, as in: It is illegal to exceed the speed limit.
- *Accept:* To agree to take, as in: I accept the terms of your offer.
- *Except:* Excluding, as in: I knew all the answers on the test, except the last one.
- *Access:* Permission to go in or to approach, as in: No one has access to my private files but me.
- *Excess:* More than enough, as in: We gave our excess fruit to our neighbors.
- *Expand:* Enlarge, as in: One reason for a business to have a Web site is to expand its market.
- *Expend:* Pay out money, as in: Because they neglected to expend any money or time on marketing their business, they soon went bankrupt.
- *Expansive:* Broad, as in: Their expansive front lawn was the envy of the neighborhood.
- *Expensive:* Costing a lot of money, as in: A large front lawn can be expensive when you add up the water bills, fertilizer bills, and energy consumed in mowing it regularly.
- *Expatiate:* Write or speak in great detail, as in: Please forgive me if I expatiate, but this is my favorite topic.
- *Expiate:* Atone for or make amends for, as in: She devoted her life to charity to try to expiate the wrongs of her youth.
- *Extant:* Still existing, as in: The museum has the last extant copy of the manuscript.

— *Extent:* The limit to which something extends, as in: The extent of the Universe seems to grow as our ability to make better telescopes grows.

AVOIDABLE ENGLISH ERRORS

Avoidable English Errors are so many that we have to spend a lot of time to know.English can be a tricky language to master. There are a number of words that sound the same but mean different things or those are spelled differently, and it's easy to get confused. Another problem area is when people translate sentences. Sentences in English are structured differently and a direct translation is often incorrect and can even be misleading. To help you improve your English-speaking skills, we have added this page with many more Avoidable English Errors.

— Wrong: Myself Sunil Kumar

— Correct: I am Sunil Kumar

Many people believe the word MYSELF makes the statement formal. It's actually incorrect in this context.

— Wrong: You will surely get more better.

— Correct: You will surely get better.

English has a few adjectives of which comparative and superlative forms are irregular. The adjective Good turns into Better in the comparative and BEST in the superlative. The word MORE should not be included.

— Wrong: I will return back.

— Correct: I will return.

If you will return to something, it means you will come back to it. Therefore, the word BACK is not needed.

— Wrong: I will talk to the principle of this college.

— Correct: I will talk to the principal of this college.

The words PRINCIPLE and PRINCIPAL are often confused. Every principal should have principles is an easy way to remember the difference.

Another one of those Avoidable English Errors is:

Wrong: I didn't went to New York in the last year.

— Correct: I didn't go to New York in the last year.

— Wrong: I did called her last week.

— Correct: I did call her last week.

Question: Have you ever been to the US?

— Wrong: I go to the US last year.

— Correct: I did go to the US last year.

Question: Didn't you eat last night?

— Wrong: I did ate.

— Correct: I did eat.

DID indicates that the action has happened in the past. Hence, the other verb should be in present tense.

Also, DID / DO are used to stress a point.

For example:

Question: Did you go to America last year?

Correct: I did.

Question: Does anybody here speak French?

Answer: I do.

Another one of those Avoidable English Errors is:

There is a mistake many of us make while using the present tense. There are two forms of the present tense.

— The simple present tense
— The present continuous tense

The simple present tense is used for two main types of action:Habits—Actions which happen regularly (every day, every week, etc.)

— Example - Sneha goes to class every day.
— Explanation - Doing something every day makes it a habit.

States of being - Things which do not often change (opinions, conditions, etc.)

— Example - Pramod lives in Mumbai.
— Explanation - This is a state of being, because it will not change (or change infrequently).

The present continuous tense is used for two main types of action:

A temporary action happening now (but it will stop in the future).

— Example - It's raining outside.
— Explanation - It's raining right now, but it may stop soon.

A definite plan for the future. Something we intend to do, usually in the near future.

- Example - The Olympics are taking place here next year.
- Explanation - This is already certain.

Examples

- Wrong: I am getting up every day at 6 am.
- Correct: I get up every day at 6 am.
- Wrong: I have a party next week.
- Correct: I am having a party next week.
- Wrong: If you are not esperience, try to get help.
- Correct: If you have no experience, try to get help.
- Wrong: Suppose if you knows the value, then why you fear to buy?
- Correct: If you know the value, why are you afraid to buy?
- Wrong: Myself working in a MNC.
- Correct: I am working in a MNC.

Another one of those Avoidable English Errors is:

- Wrong: He is calling to you.

The TO is not needed in this statment. You could either remove the TO or replace it with FOR.

- Correct: He is calling you.
- Wrong: Say me the truth!

This is especially prevalent in Andhra Pradesh. It should be TELL.

- Correct: Tell me the truth.
- Wrong: The real fact is that you are not married.

This is redundant, because a fact is true or provable. Therefore, all facts are real.

— Correct: The fact is that you are not married.

— Wrong: I am having a lovely family.

This type of error is easy to hear in India. We use the present continuous tense in place of the present simple tense.

— Correct: I have a lovely family.

Another one of those Avoidable English Errors is:

— Wrong: This vehicle is dead cheap.

When a product is very cheap, a lot of us say it is dead cheap. Actually, the phrase is DIRT CHEAP.

— Correct: This vehicle is dirt cheap.

— Wrong: It will be a very cut and right report.

The proper phrase is CUT AND DRY or CUT AND DRIED. It means that something is settled or routine.

— Correct: It will be a very cut and dried report.

— Wrong: If you can do, do. If you cannot, admit yourself.

— Correct: If you can do it, do it. If you cannot do it, admit it to yourself.

Another one of those Avoidable English Errors is:

— Wrong: What O'clock you are coming for dinner?

— Correct: What time are you coming for dinner?

— Wrong: Take this letter and post yourself.

— Correct: Please take this letter and post it yourself.

— Wrong: Can you capable work this Sunday?

— Correct: Are you able to work this Sunday?

— Wrong: Both the three of you to do field duty.

- Correct: All three of you, go do field duty.
- Wrong: Mind me to get some flowers this evening.
- Correct: Please remind me to get some flowers this evening.
- Wrong: Udupi Hotel fooding is not good.
- Correct: The food at Udupi Hotel is not good.

9

Vocabulary Building

When you leave school or college, someone will inevitably point out that this is not the end and that it is only the beginning. Of course the speaker is right. No educative process is the end. It is always the beginning of more education, more learning and more living. And that is the case here. What has happened to you as a result of your reaction to the material and suggestion in this site is only the beginning of your development.

To stop increasing your vocabulary is to stop your intellectual growth. You will wish, we are sure, to continue to growing intellectually as long as you remain alive. And with the momentum that your weeks of hard work have provided, continuing will not be at all difficult.

Step one: You must become actively receptive to new words: Words won't come chasing after you. You must train yourself to be on a constant lookout, in reading and listening for any words that other people know and you do not.

Step two: You must read more: As an adult, you will find most of the sources of your supply of new words in books and magazines. Is your reading today largely restricted only to the quick perusal of daily news papers? Then you will have to change your habits. If your aim is to have superior vocabulary, you will have to make the time to read at least one book and several magazines every week. Not this week and the next week, but every week for the rest of your life. I have never met a single person who possessed a rich vocabulary and who was not also an omnivorous reader.

Step Three: You must learn to add to your own vocabulary the new words you meet in your reading: When you see an unfamiliar word in a book or in a magazine, do not skip over it impatiently. Instead pause for a moment and say it to yourself. Get used to its sound and appearance. Then puzzle out its possible meaning in the context of the sentence. Whether you come to the right conclusion or not, whether indeed you are able to come to any intelligent conclusion at all is of no importance. What is important is that, by that process, becoming superconscious of that word. As a result, you will suddenly notice that this very word pops up unexpectedly again and again in all you reading. For now your mind has been alerted to notice it. And of course after you have seen it a few times, you will know fairly accurately not only what it means but the many ways in which it can be used.

Step Four: You must open your mind to new ideas: Every word you see is the translation of new idea. Think for few minutes of the areas of human knowledge that may possibly be unknown to you—Psychology, semantics, science, art, music, management, etc... Then attack one of these areas methodically, by reading books on that particular subject. In every field, form the simplest to the most abstruse, there are several books for the average, untrained lay reader that will give you both a good grasp of the subject and at the same time add vocabularies because they are required to expose themselves constantly to new areas of learning. You must do the same.

Step Five: You must set a goal: If you do nothing about your vocabulary, you will learn, at most, twenty-five to fifty new words in the next twelve months. In conscious efforts, you can learn several thousands. Set your self a goal of finding several new words every day. This may sound ambitious, but you will discove as soon as you start actively looking for new words in your reading, and actively doing reading of a more challenging type, that new words are all around you. That is, if you are ready for them. And understand this. Vocabulary building snowballs. The results of each new day search will be greater and greater- once you provide the necessary initial push, once you gain momentum, once you become addicted to looking for new words, for finding new words and for taking possession of new words. And this one addiction well worth cultivating.

MAKING IT PERSONAL

Everyone-From Beginning Learners in English to veterans in journalism-knows the frustration of not having the right word immediately available in that lexicon one carries between one's ears. Sometimes it's a matter of not being able to recall the right word; sometimes we never knew it. It is also frustrating to read a newspaper or homework assignment and run across words whose meanings elude us. Language, after all, is power. When your children get in trouble fighting with the neighbours' children, and your neighbours call your children little twerps and you call their children nefarious miscreants-well, the battle is over and they didn't stand a chance. Building a vocabulary that is adequate to the needs of one's reading and self-expression has to be a personal goal for every writer and speaker.

Using some durable piece of paper-white construction paper or the insides of the ripped-off covers of old notebooks-begin to write down words in small but readable script that you discover in your reading that you can't define. Read journals and newspapers that challenge you in terms of vocabulary. Pursue words actively and become alert to words that you simply overlooked in the past. Write down the words in one column; then, later, when you have a dictionary at your disposal, write down a common definition of the word; in a third column, write a brief sentence using the word, underlined.

Carry this paper or cardboard with you always. In the pauses of your busy day-when you're sitting on the bus, in the dentist's office, during commercials-take out the paper and review your vocabulary words until you feel comfortable that you would recognise (and be able to use) these words the next time you see them. The amazing thing is that you will see the words again-even "nefarious miscreants," and probably sooner than you thought. In fact, you might well discover that the words you've written down are rather common. What's happening is not that, all of a sudden, people are using words you never saw before, but that you are now reading and using words that you had previously ignored.

USING EVERY RESOURCE

Most bookstores carry books on building a more powerful vocabulary, some of them with zany names such as Thirty Days to a More Powerful Vocabulary. If you've got money to spare or if they're on sale, buy them and use them: they can't hurt. Books that group words according to what they have in common-more in meaning than in spelling-are especially useful. Newspapers often carry brief daily articles that explore the meanings of words and phrases. These articles often emphasize peculiar words that won't find themselves into your working vocabulary, but they can still be fun. Often you'll find that learning one new word leads to other new words, little constellations of meaning that keep your brain cells active and hungry for more. Make reading these articles one of your daily habits, an addiction, even.

Play dictionary games with your family in which someone uses the dictionary to find a neat word and writes down the real definition and everyone else writes down a fake (and funny) definition.

A thesaurus is like a dictionary except that it groups words within constellations of meaning. It is often useful in discovering just the right word you need to express what you want to say. Make sure you correctly understand the definition of a word (by using a dictionary) before using it in some important paper or report.

Your bookstore salesperson can provide plenty of examples of an inexpensive thesaurus. The online Merriam Webster's WWWebster Dictionary has access to both an extensive dictionary and a hyperlinked thesaurus. Links allow you to go conveniently back and forth between the dictionary and the thesaurus.

If you have a speedy computer processor and a fast hookup to the internet. Once the programme is entirely loaded, type in a word that you would like to see "visualised," hit the return key, and a construct of verbal connections will float across the screen. Click on any of the words within that construct and a new pattern of connections will emerge. Try the Visual Thesaurus with several different kinds of words-verbs, adverbs, nouns, adjectives-and try adjusting some of the various controls on the bottom of the window.

When people use a word that puzzles you, ask what it means! You'll find that most instructors, especially, are not in the least bothered by such questions-in fact, they're probably pleased that you're paying such close attention-but if they do seem bothered, write down the word and look it up later, before the context of the word evaporates.

KNOWING THE ROOTS

At least half of the words in the English language are derived from Greek and Latin roots. Knowing these roots helps us to grasp the meaning of words before we look them up in the dictionary. It also helps us to see how words are often arranged in families with similar characteristics. For instance, we know that sophomores are students in their second year of college or high school. What does it mean, though, to be sophomoric? The "sopho" part of the word comes from the same Greek root that gives us philosophy, which we know means "love of knowledge."

The "ic" ending is sometimes added to adjectival words in English, but the "more" part of the word comes from the same Greek root that gives us moron. Thus sophomores are people who think they know a lot but really don't know much about anything, and a sophomoric act is typical of a "wise fool," a "smart-ass"!

Let's explore further. Going back to philosophy, we know the "sophy" part is related to knowledge and the "phil" part is related to love (because we know that Philadelphia is the City of Brotherly Love and that a philodendron loves shady spots). What, then, is philanthropy? "Phil" is still love, and "anthropy" comes from the same Greek root that gives us anthropology, which is the study ("logy," we know, means study of any kind) of anthropos, humankind. So a philanthropist must be someone who loves humans and does something about it-like giving money to find a cure for cancer or to build a Writing Center for the local community college.

(And an anthropoid, while we're at it, is an animal who walks like a human being.) Learning the roots of our language can even be fun!

Some common Greek and Latin roots:

Root (source)	Meaning	English words
aster, astr (G)	star	astronomy, astrology
audi (L)	to hear	audible, auditorium
bene (L)	good, well	benefit, benevolent
bio (G)	life	biology, autobiography
dic, dict (L)	to speak	dictionary, dictator
fer (L)	to carry	transfer, referral
fix (L)	to fasten	fix, suffix, affix
geo (G)	earth	geography, geology
graph (G)	to write	graphic, photography
jur, just (L)	law	jury, justice
log, logue (G)	word, thought, speech	monolog(ue), astrology, biology, neologism
luc (L)	light	lucid, translucent
manu (L)	hand	manual, manuscript
meter, metr (G)	measure	metric, thermometer

op, oper (L)	work	operation, operator
path (G)	feeling	pathetic, sympathy, empathy
ped (G)	child	pediatrics, pedophile
phil (G)	love	philosophy, Anglophile
phys (G)	body, nature	physical, physics
scrib, script (L)	to write	scribble, manuscript
tele (G)	far off	telephone, television
ter, terr (L)	earth	territory, extraterrestrial
vac (L)	empty	vacant, vacuum, evacuate
verb (L)	word	verbal, verbose
vid, vis (L)	to see	video, vision, television

LEARNING PREFIXES AND SUFFIXES

Knowing the Greek and Latin roots of several prefixes and suffixes (beginning and endings attached to words) can also help us determine the meaning of words. Ante, for instance, means before, and if we connect bellum with belligerant to figure out the connection with war, we'll know that antebellum refers to the period before war.

Prefixes showing quantity

Meaning	Prefixes in English Words
half	semiannual, hemisphere
one	unicycle, monarchy, monorail
two	binary, bimonthly, dilemma, dichotomy
hundred	century, centimeter, hectoliter
thousand	millimeter, kilometer

Prefixes showing negation

Meaning	Prefixes in English Words
without, no, not	asexual, anonymous, illegal, immoral, invalid, irreverent, unskilled
not, absence of, opposing, against	nonbreakable, antacid, antipathy, contradict
opposite to, complement to	counterclockwise, counterweight
do the opposite of, remove, reduce	dehorn, devitalise, devalue
do the opposite deprive of	disestablish, disarm
wrongly, bad	misjudge, misdeed

Prefixes showing time

Meaning	Prefixes in English Words
before	antecedent, forecast, precede, prologue
after	postwar
again	rewrite, redundant

Prefixes showing direction or position

above, over	supervise, supererogatory
across, over	transport, translate
below, under	infrasonic, infrastructure, subterranean, hypodermic
in front of	proceed, prefix
behind	recede
out of	erupt, explicit, ecstasy
into	injection, immerse, encourage, empower
around	circumnavigate, perimeter
with	coexist, colloquy, communicate, consequence, correspond, sympathy, synchronize

Suffixes, on the other hand, modify the meaning of a word and frequently determine its function within a sentence. Take the noun nation, for example. With suffixes, the word becomes the adjective national, the adverb nationally, and the verb nationalise.

See what words you can come up with that use the following suffixes.

— Typical noun suffixes are -ence, -ance, -or, -er, -ment, -list, -ism, -ship, -ency, -sion, -tion, -ness, -hood, -dom

— Typical verb suffixes are -en, -ify, -ize, -ate

— Typical adjective suffixes are -able, -ible, -al, -tial, -tic, -ly, -ful, -ous, -tive, -less, -ish, -ulent

— The adverb suffix is -ly (although not all words that end in -ly are adverbs-like friendly)

USING THE DICTIONARY

The dictionary should be one of the most often used books in your home. (We'll allow room for sacred texts here.) Place the dictionary somewhere so that you can find it immediately and use it often. If you do your reading and homework in the kitchen and the dictionary is on a shelf in the den or bedroom, it's too tempting to say "I'll look it up next time."

The home dictionary should be large enough to contain much more than just spellings. It should contain extensive definitions, word origins, and notes on usage. Carrying in your purse or backpack a pocket dictionary with more concise definitions is also a good idea. Get in the habit of turning to it often. A well worn dictionary is a beautiful thing.

USING THE INTERNET

You can use the internet as an aid to vocabulary development by exploring the abundant opportunities for reading available on the World Wide Web. Capital Community College maintains an extensive list of online newspapers and commentary magazines. Choose magazines such as Atlantic and Mother Jones that challenge your mind and your vocabulary with full-text articles. At least once a week read a major article with the purpose of culling from it some vocabulary words that are unfamiliar to you.

Vocabulary University is a new online resource for working on groups of related vocabulary words in a puzzle format. Vocabulary U., a graphically rich Web site, is broken into beginning, intermediate, and college-level work. Vocabulary for English Language Learners is a treasury and nicely organised resources for ESL students. It is maintained by the College of Arts & Sciences of Ohio University.

There are also at least two services that send you an e-mail message every day with a new word-with definitions, pronunciation guides, and examples of its use. Get in the habit of reading these messages regularly. Print out the words and definitions you think will be really useful, or write them down and carry them around with you on your personal vocabulary builder.

Bibliography

Aaron, Jane E. *The Little, Brown Essential Handbook for Writers.* New York, Longman, 2003. 251p.

Alexander, L.G. 1988. *Longman English Grammar.* London: Longman.

Bauer, Laurie. (1983). *English word-formation.* Cambridge: Cambridge University Press.

Brazil, David. 1985. *The Communicative Value of Intonation in English.* Discourse Monograph No. 8, University of Birmingham: English Language Research.

Celce-Murcia, M.; & Larsen-Freeman, D. *The grammar book: An ESL/EFL teacher's course.*

Coulthard, Malcolm. 1992. "The Significance of Intonation in Discourse." in *Advances in Spoken Discourse Analysis,* ed. Malcolm Coulthard. London and New York: Routledge, pp.35-49.

Delahunty, Gerald P. and James J. Garvey. *Language, Grammar, & Communication: A Course for Teachers of English.* St.Louis: McGraw-Hill, 1994.

Greenbaum, Sidney. 1989. *A College Grammar of English.* New York and London: Longman.

Halliday, M. A. K. (2004). *Introduction to functional grammar* (3rd. ed.). London: Hodder Arnold.

John B. Carroll, eds., *Language Comprehension and the Acquisition of Knowledge.* Washington, D.C.: V. H. Winston.

Leech, Geoffrey and Jan Svartvik. 1975. *A Communicative Grammar of English.* London: Longman.

Martinet, André. 1962. *A Functional View of Language.* Oxford: The Clarendon Press.

Muir, James. 1972. *A Modern Approach to English Grammar: An Introduction to Systemic Grammar.* London: B.T. Batsford, Ltd.

Newby, Michael. 1987. *The Structure of English: A Handbook of English Grammar.* Cambridge: Cambridge University Press.

Plag, Ingo. (2003). *Word-formation in English*. Cambridge: Cambridge University Press.

Quirk, Randolph, Sidney Greenbaum, Geoffrey Leech, and Jan Svartvik. 1972. *A Grammar of Contemporary English*. London: Longman.

Roberts, Paul. 1954. *Understanding Grammar*. New York: Harper and Row.

Strang, Barbara M. H. (1968). *Modern English structure* (2nd ed.). London: Arnold.

Strunk, William, Jr. and E.B. White. *Elements of Style*,. 3rd Ed., Boston: Allyn and Bacon, 1979.

Taylor, John R. 1995. *Linguistic Categorization: Prototypes in Linguistic Theory*. Oxford: Clarendon Press

Vitale, Edmund, Jr. *Thinking Your Way Through English Grammar*. Clearwater, Florida: H & H Publishing, 1991.

Yule, George. 1996. *The Study of Language, Second Edition*. New York: Cambridge University Press.